I0825311

A DAY IN PENANG

A DAY IN PENANG

A Malaysian cookbook

Aim Aris &
Ahmad Salim

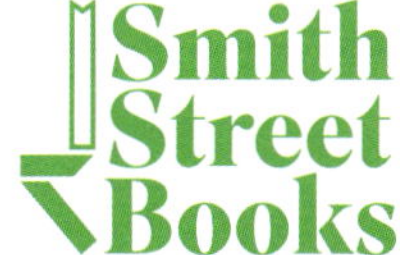

INTRODUCTION

Walking through the streets of George Town, Penang's capital city located on the northeastern corner of the island, you are surrounded by the heritage buildings that signify the city's colonial past. A historical hub of different ethnicities and cultures, the island of Penang is the oldest of the British Straits Settlements in Southeast Asia, and today it entwines this colonial heritage with 21st century living.

In Malaysia, Penang is well known as a food-lover's destination, evident by the many specialty dishes you can only find in the region. Rich in history and tradition, every cuisine – Malay, Chinese, Peranakan, Indian, among others – are showcased harmoniously beside one another, culminating into what we now call Penang cuisine. As you explore the winding lanes of George Town, armed with a camera and a hungry tummy, it is impossible not to be drawn into the multiple restaurants and food markets this vibrant city has to offer.

Penang's colonial history dates back to the 16th century, when Portuguese traders from Goa, India, came across a small island while sailing to the Far East in search of spices. The island soon became a stop-off point for traders travelling along the Maritime Silk Road in need of fresh water supplies. The traders named the island Pulo Pinoam. In 1786, the British explorer Captain Francis Light took possession of the island from the Sultan of Kedah (a Muslim dynasty located on the Malaysian Peninsula) in exchange for British protection against their enemies, namely from Burma (Myanmar) and Siam (Thailand).

Light renamed the island Prince of Wales Island, although the locals referred to it as Pulau Pinang (*pinang* being the local word for the betel nut, which grows abundantly on the island). Under Light's administrative and development policies, many traders flocked to the province, and the newly founded city of George Town soon became an entrepôt serving the trade routes between Southeast Asia, East Asia, South Asia, West Asia and Europe. In addition to the many goods that exchanged hands on Penang, the island also exported tin, spices, rattans, gold, ivory, ebony and pepper. Light wanted to transform Penang into a 'second Moluccas' (a reference to the Maluku Islands controlled at the time by the Dutch East India Company), by introducing peppercorn vines from the Indonesian province of Aceh in order to reinforce the power of the British East India Company against its rival. The first seedlings were successfully planted in the late 1790s and Penang's pepper soon became a highly sought after crop, comparable in quality to the Malabar pepper. This continued until the late 1860s when nutmeg and clove reached peak production and overtook pepper as the largest export crops.

As a result of British and Dutch colonial rule in India and Malacca, Indian and Chinese immigrants started settling in Penang. Over time, smaller communities from Eurasia, Burma, Siam, Aceh, Saudi Arabia, Armenia, Japan and Europe also began to arrive, bringing with them their cultures, languages, food knowledge and ingredients, which contributed to the multi-ethnic and multicultural Penang that exists today.

The popular saying 'you are what you eat' sits close to the hearts of many Penangites, for whom food also carries cultural and religious symbolism. Likewise, food has evolved as a cultural identity that represents people and their customs. Nowhere is this more apparent than in George Town, which encapsulates the multiculturalism of Penang through its diverse food culture. Home to some of Penang's best restaurants, cafes and hawker stalls, this vibrant city is the culinary heartbeat of Penang. You only have to visit Little India, Burma Street and Chulia Street to understand why the city is the street-food capital of Malaysia. Equipped with hot woks and speed, hawkers work fast with high flames and incredible heat, preparing dishes, such as *Char kuey teow* (see page 142) and *Mee goreng Mamak* (see page 156), for hungry patrons.

There are also many markets to visit, day or night, and here you'll find locals catching up over a steaming bowl of noodles or a plate of curry and rice. It's also where people go to source fresh produce and the catch-of-the-day from the island's fishermen. One of the biggest hawker centres is Cecil Market, which combines both a wet market and food court, and it is a must visit while in Penang. Here, you will find many local dishes, such as *Kuey teow th'ng* (Flat rice noodle soup, see page 79), *Pasembur* (Malaysian-Indian salad, see page 82), *Hokkien mee* and *Nyonya kuis* (Peranakan cakes). The Air Itam Market is also hugely popular among Penangites, and here you can buy everything under one roof, from clothing to local produce. The highlight, however, is the array of delicious street foods, from *Roti canai* (see page 20) and curry noodles to *Char koay kak* and *Asam laksa* (see page 54). Come evening, the night markets are equally exciting, and in Penang there is a night market for every day of the week. With a long stretch of hawker and trader stalls, you will find endless selections of street foods, such as satays, *Lok lok* (see page 150), *Belacan* fried chicken (see page 146) and *Popiah* (fresh spring rolls). Some of the famous night markets you can visit include the Macallum Street Night Market, Tanjung Bungah Night Market, Farlim Night Market, Batu Ferringhi Night Market and Jelutong Night Market.

Although centuries old, Penang's food scene is never stagnant, and the island's food culture continues to evolve, thanks in part to the many new indoor restaurants and cafes that cater to younger crowds looking to indulge in cuisines beyond Malaysia's borders. But regardless of where you are in Penang, George Town or Gurney Drive, Balik Pulau or Batu Ferringhi, there will always be passionate and dedicated cooks working hard to make the food their patrons love. It is this dedication and passion that helps make Penang's cuisine unique, and keeps locals and visitors alike always hungry for more.

VA

CHEF'S NOTES

Santan, or coconut milk, is one of the most important ingredients in Malaysian cuisine, particularly in Malay, Indian and Peranakan dishes. Coconut milk is used in both sweet and savoury recipes throughout this book, where it adds creaminess and flavour to curries and desserts.

Gula melaka, or palm sugar, is derived from the sap of coconut palms, which grow abundantly in Penang. It is generally less sweet than refined white or brown sugar, and it has a rich complexity that exhibits hints of sourness, smoke, chocolate, caramel, butterscotch or coffee, or a combination of these flavours.

Pandan is a long, slender, fragrant green leaf that is widely used as a natural food flavouring and colouring in Malaysian cooking. Dubbed as the 'Asian vanilla', some describe pandan as nutty and botanical, while others say it has hints of rose, almond and, as suggested, vanilla.

Belacan, or fermented shrimp paste, is a staple ingredient used to make sambal or added to stir-fried dishes. Made using dried shrimp, *belacan* has a salty-umami taste. Roasting it over a high flame or in the oven before adding it to your cooking will help enhance its flavour.

Chilli is another indispensable ingredient in Malaysian cuisine. The most commonly used chillies are dried chillies, long red chillies and bird's eye chillies; the latter being the spiciest. Dried chillies are milder, but more flavourful, making them the chilli of choice for sambal-based dishes, due to their rich red hue and stronger taste.

The most commonly used spices are cinnamon, cardamom, cloves and star anise. In Malaysia, these spices are called '*rempah empat beradik*' or 'four siblings' spices' because they are nearly always used together to flavour curries, soups and rice dishes.

Malaysian curry powder is what sets traditional Malaysian curries apart from other Asian curries. The ratio of spices used in the mixture will differ depending on the type of curry you are making: usually seafood, meat or chicken. Regardless, the 'four siblings' spices' (see above) are always present in all curry powders.

Rice is a staple for Malaysians where it is considered an 'all-day' dish. The most common types of rice are jasmine and basmati. Jasmine rice is less starchy and, therefore, usually paired with curries, soups or stir-fries. Basmati rice, with its excellent cooking quality and flavour, is preferred when cooking flavoured rice dishes, such as *Nasi tomato* (Tomato rice, see page 95) or *Nasi dalca* (Dal rice, see page 92).

Tamarind is abundant in Penang and it is widely used in many of Malaysia's signature dishes. It can be purchased in three forms: tamarind paste, which needs to be soaked in hot water before adding the liquid to your cooking; dried tamarind slices for a lighter tamarind flavour, and concentrated tamarind, which requires only a small amount when adding to dishes.

No Malaysian kitchen is complete without a wok. It is used to make stir-fries, such as *Char kuey teow* (Stir-fried flat rice noodles, see page 142), and any dishes that are sauce- or soup-based. Woks enable high-heat cooking, known as '*wok hei*' or 'the breath of the wok', which gives dishes their signature smoky flavour.

Steamers are another essential piece of equipment widely used in Malaysian cooking. Back in the day, most Malaysian households did not have access to an oven, which is why many desserts and sweet treats are steamed, unlike Western-style desserts.

The recipes in this cookbook serve as a guideline, but feel free to adjust levels of spiciness or seasoning to suit your preference. To cook like a true Malaysian, the principle of *agak-agak* (to estimate or guess) is very important. The ability to ensure that the flavours are a balance of spicy, sweet, sour, salty and umami is essential. You are welcome to add, omit or substitute some of the ingredients, depending on what's available to you or your dietary requirements, but most importantly, have fun and experiment with the dishes that you love.

MILO
Penang
White Coffee

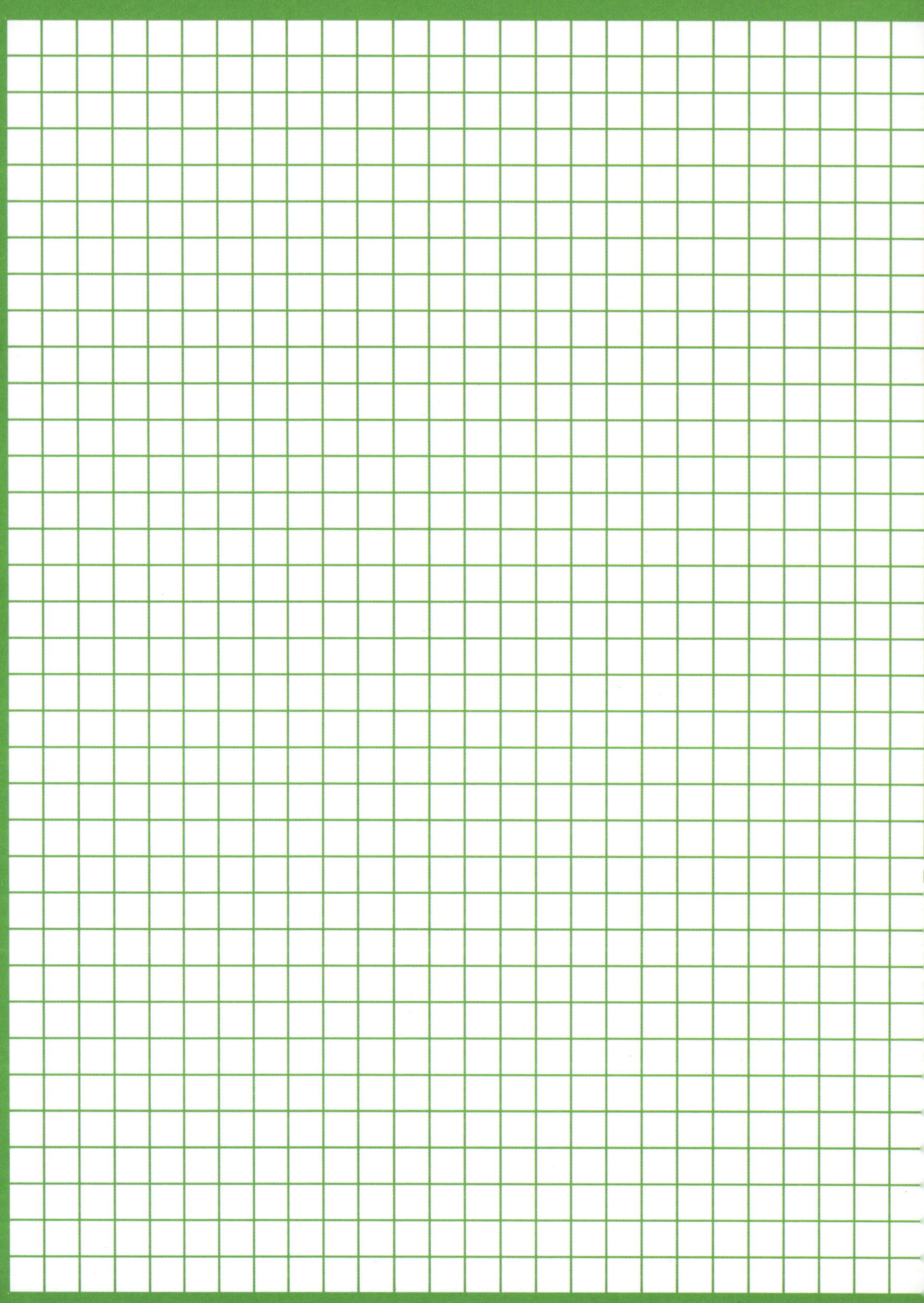

EARLY

MAMA's
PNQ
8265

As the old adage goes, breakfast is the most important meal of the day, and Penangites eat breakfast like true kings. Since many locals start their morning as early as dawn, to go to school or work, weekday breakfasts need to be fast, convenient and filling enough to get them up and running until lunchtime. Traditional *kopitiams* (coffee shops) are set up early, with hawkers selling a variety of local delicacies, such as *Nasi lemak* (see page 28), *roti bakar* (toasts) and *kuihs* (sweet and savoury bites) to patrons who either prefer to dine in or *tapau* (take away) their breakfast.

Younger crowds often kickstart their mornings with a bit of cafe-hopping around Penang. These days, specialty coffee, rather than the classic kopi 'O' (black coffee), and Western-style breakfasts are the go-to over traditional Malaysian fare. With artisan bakeries popping up across George Town and Pulau Tikus, many are swapping *roti bakar* for sourdough and pastries, preferring to sit down, chat and ease into the day.

Weekend mornings in Penang tend to start a little slower, with whole families heading out for breakfast at their favourite restaurants or hawker stalls before spending time at the beach or a park. Sometimes, one person will make the morning market run, picking up a variety of breakfast bites to enjoy as a leisurely meal at home.

Ask any Penangite and they'll have their go-to breakfast spot. For us, it's the charcoal-grilled *roti bakar* and kopi 'O' at Toh Soon Café on Campbell Street, or the spicy *nasi lemak* wrapped in banana leaves from a vendor at Sri Weld Food Court in George Town. And if we're feeling extra hungry, we'll make the trip to Gelugor for a hearty spread of traditional Malay-style breakfasts at Astaka Taman Tun Sardon.

HAINANESE-STYLE KAYA TOAST AND HALF-BOILED EGG

Kaya toast is a popular breakfast dish served in *kopitiams* (coffee shops) all over Penang. In many of the *kopitiams* the Hainanese bread used in the dish is made inhouse, traditionally toasted by hand over charcoal to add a lovely smoky flavour to the bread. The method in the recipe below offers a nice alternative for those making it at home. Another secret to good *kaya* toast is the *kaya* itself (a sweet coconut jam), as well as a slice of cold butter to balance the sweet-salty taste of the toast. Serve with a cup of coffee – preferably kopi 'O' (black coffee).

SERVES 4

4 eggs, at room temperature
light soy sauce, to taste
ground white pepper
8 slices of soft white bread/ Hainanese bread, crusts removed
Hainanese *kaya* (Caramel coconut jam, see page 191), for spreading
4 thin slices salted butter
black coffee, to serve

1 Bring a saucepan of water to the boil, then remove from the heat. Using a spoon, lower the eggs into the water, then cover with a lid and let the residual heat gently cook the eggs for 7 minutes. Remove the eggs from the water, then gently crack each egg into a small bowl, scooping out any remaining egg white clinging to the shell. Add a few drops of soy sauce and a dash of ground white pepper.

2 Grill the bread in a hot frying pan or under a hot oven grill (broiler) until well toasted on both sides. Spread a nice layer of *kaya* over each slice, and arrange the cold butter on half the toast slices. Top with the remaining slices, *kaya* side down, and cut in half.

3 Serve the warm toast with the half-boiled eggs and black coffee. Dip the toast into the egg for the best experience!

ROTI CANAI

MALAYSIAN-STYLE PARATHA ROTI

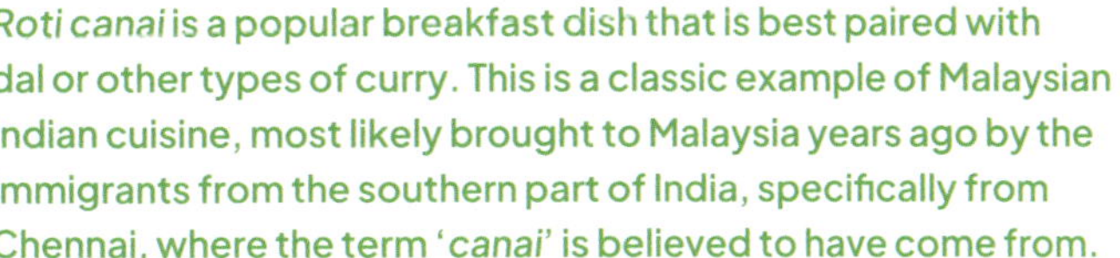

Roti canai is a popular breakfast dish that is best paired with dal or other types of curry. This is a classic example of Malaysian Indian cuisine, most likely brought to Malaysia years ago by the immigrants from the southern part of India, specifically from Chennai, where the term '*canai*' is believed to have come from.

In Penang, Mamak (Malaysian-Indian) stalls selling *roti canai* are easily found and usually operate 24 hours a day, every day – making it a versatile and cheap all-day snack and a great meeting point when you're catching up with friends.

SERVES 4

vegetable oil, for coating

Dough

- 450 g (3 cups) plain (all-purpose) flour
- 125 ml (½ cup) vegetable oil, plus extra to coat
- 1 tablespoon sugar
- 1 teaspoon salt
- 250 ml (1 cup) lukewarm water

Note

Once you have made the roti you can add any number of extra ingredients. The two variations most commonly ordered by locals are *roti telur* (egg roti) and *roti banjir* (flooded roti).

To make *roti telur*: at step 6, after placing the flattened spiralled dough in the pan, crack an egg beside the roti, then place the cooked roti on top of the egg. Once the egg is cooked, flip the roti and proceed with the remaining steps.

To make *roti banjir*: at step 7, after giving the roti a quick 'clap', cut or shred it into bite-sized pieces, then pour over your choice of curry or dal until the roti is completely covered.

1 To make the dough, place the flour and oil in a bowl and mix well. Dilute the sugar and salt with 2 tablespoons of lukewarm water, then pour it into the flour mixture. Add the remaining water and stir until the mixture is well combined.

2 Using the '3 minutes knead then 2 minutes rest' method, knead the dough with clean hands until it is smooth and no longer sticky. This is to stretch the gluten in the flour and give the desired texture of *roti canai*.

3 Divide the dough into eight portions and roll into small balls. Roll the balls in oil until well coated and rest for at least an hour, or preferably overnight.

4 To '*canai*' (flatten the dough), flip a 32 cm (12½ in) round tray over as you'll be using the underside (a pizza tray is ideal). Take one dough ball and press it firmly onto the tray with your palm. Working your way around, gently pull the dough towards the edge of tray, keeping the shape as round as possible. Continue until the dough has almost completely covered the tray.

5 Lift one edge of the dough and carefully pull it off the tray. Roll it up, then coil it into a spiral shape, then gently press down on it and set aside. Repeat with the remaining dough balls. Sprinkle the dough with oil and rest for 3–5 minutes.

6 Heat a clean frying pan over medium heat. Working with one piece at a time, flatten the rested dough once again, then place it in the pan and cook for 1–2 minutes until the base is lightly brown and crisp. Flip the roti over and cook until cooked through and lightly brown on both sides.

7 Remove the roti from the pan and give it a light 'clap' between your hands. Repeat with the remaining dough. Serve warm with curry, dal, sugar or enjoy it plain.

PUTU MAYAM

MALAYSIAN-STYLE STRING HOPPERS

If you stroll around Chowrasta Market or Ayer Itam Market, you will always find mobile street vendors selling *putu mayam*. This simple dish can be traced back to southern India, where the *putu mayam* is quite similar to *idiyappam* (string hoppers). However, the *putu mayam* in Malaysia is usually eaten cold with freshly grated coconut and brown sugar – an influence from Kerala Indians who migrated to Penang many years back.

You will need a string hopper maker to make this recipe. You can buy them online or from Indian grocery stores.

SERVES 4

- 3–4 banana leaves
- 1 tablespoon vegetable oil
- 1 teaspoon salt
- 350 g (2 cups) rice flour
- freshly grated coconut, mixed with a pinch of salt, and shaved *gula melaka* (palm sugar) or soft brown sugar, to serve

1 Rinse the banana leaves and wipe them clean, then cut into 12–16 × 7.5 cm (3 in) circles and brush with a little oil. Set aside.

2 Bring 500 ml (2 cups) water to the boil in a saucepan, then add the salt and remaining oil and stir well. Remove the pan from the heat and gradually add the rice flour, stirring constantly, until it becomes a soft dough. While the dough is still hot, carefully add a small portion of dough (enough to fill the maker) to the *idiyappam*/string hopper maker, then gently press the dough onto a piece of banana leaf. Repeat with the remaining dough and banana leaf circles.

3 Working in batches, add the *putu mayam* to a steamer basket and steam for 2–3 minutes until cooked through. Cover the steamer lid with a tea (dish) towel to stop them going soggy.

4 Gently remove the *putu mayam* from the steamer and allow to cool, then serve with grated coconut and sugar.

Notes

For green *putu mayam*, blend 4–5 pandan leaves with 500 ml (2 cups) water. Strain before continuing with step 2 of the method.

You can buy fresh banana leaves from your local Asian grocer or supermarket. Frozen banana leaves can also be used, but you'll need to let them thaw at room temperature first, then rinse and wipe clean before using.

ROTI JALA

LACY PANCAKES

Roti jala literally means 'net bread' in Malay, due to its lacy or net-like appearance. Traditionally, *roti jala* was offered during festive seasons or *kenduri* (Malay community gatherings) but these days it is very common to see them sold by street hawkers as a popular breakfast meal.

Roti jala is usually served with chicken curry but the locals also suggested we try it with a plate of *Ayam masak bawang* (Onion chicken, see page 127) from a stall located in Little India. Safe to say, the flavour combo hit the spot!

You will need a special *roti jala* cup to make these. Local Asian grocery stores that specialise in Southeast Asian ingredients normally have them, but if you can't find one, you can use any squeeze bottle – preferably with three to five nozzles, otherwise make your own by puncturing five holes in a clean coconut milk (or similar) tin.

SERVES 4

- 150 g (1 cup) plain (all-purpose) flour
- ¼ teaspoon salt
- ¼ teaspoon ground turmeric
- 1 egg
- 180 ml (¾ cup) coconut milk mixed with 180 ml (¾ cup) water
- vegetable oil, for pan-frying

1 Place all the ingredients except the oil in a clean bowl and stir until well combined. Strain the batter into another bowl. Use a stick blender if needed to get a really smooth texture.

2 Heat a medium frying pan over medium heat and lightly brush with oil.

3 Pour a ladleful of batter into a *roti jala* cup and move over the frying pan in an overlapping circular motion to create the lacy effect.

4 Leave the batter to cook until set, roughly 2 minutes, then slide the pancake onto a plate and allow to cool slightly. Fold in both sides of the pancake, then roll it up to form a neat roll. Repeat with the remaining batter. You should have enough to make about 10 pancakes.

5 Serve the *roti jala* with your choice of curry.

NASI LEMAK

COCONUT RICE

Nasi lemak is a fragrant rice dish cooked in coconut milk and pandan leaves. A basic *nasi lemak* usually comes with sambal, hard-boiled egg, sliced cucumbers, fried peanuts and fried dried anchovies, but these days just about anything goes, such as chicken rendang, cockles rendang or prawn sambal. Typically, street hawkers would wrap the *nasi lemak* in a banana leaf to make the rice more fragrant – a lovely way to awaken one's appetite in the morning. Some still do this, but many opt for brown paper as a more convenient and economical wrapping.

If you go to the many street stalls, *kopitiams* (coffee shops) or food courts around Penang you can easily buy the mini version of *nasi lemak* very cheaply, offering a quick breakfast fix for locals and tourists alike.

SERVES 4

- 400 g (2 cups) basmati or long-grain rice
- 250 ml (1 cup) coconut cream
- 5 cm (2 in) piece ginger, sliced
- 1 teaspoon salt
- 2 pandan leaves, knotted

Sambal

- 2 large red onions, sliced
- 3 garlic cloves, sliced
- 15 dried chillies, soaked in water for 15 minutes
- 30 g (1 cup) dried anchovies
- 2.5 cm (1 in) piece toasted *belacan* (shrimp paste; see page 192)
- 200 ml (7 fl oz) vegetable oil
- 2 tablespoons sugar, plus extra if needed
- 1 tablespoon tamarind paste
- salt

To serve

- hard-boiled eggs, halved, or fried eggs, sunny side up
- sliced cucumbers
- fried peanuts
- fried dried anchovies

1 To make the sambal, place the red onion, garlic, drained dried chillies, dried anchovies, *belacan* and 100 ml (3½ fl oz) of the oil in a food processor or blender and process to form a paste.

2 Pour the remaining oil into a frying pan and heat over medium heat. Add the chilli paste and cook, stirring regularly, for 4–5 minutes until it turns a darker shade of red and the oil has separated.

3 Add the sugar and cook for another minute to let it caramelise with the sambal. Add the tamarind paste and 125 ml (½ cup) water and cook, stirring, for 3 minutes or until the sambal has thickened slightly. Season to taste with salt and extra sugar if needed. Keep in mind that the sambal should be a good balance of sweet, spicy and sour flavours.

4 Wash the rice until the water runs clear, then tip it into a rice cooker. Add the coconut cream and 500 ml (2 cups) water and stir in the ginger, salt and pandan leaves. Leave to soak for 5–10 minutes, then switch the rice cooker on and cook the rice according to the manufacturer's instructions.

5 Lightly fluff up the cooked rice with a fork or a wooden spoon. Serve immediately with the sambal, egg, cucumber, peanuts and dried anchovies.

Note

The sambal will make more than is needed for this recipe. Keep the leftovers in an airtight container in the fridge for up to 5 days.

RICE

It is no secret that Malaysians love rice. It is a staple everyday ingredient, consumed for breakfast, lunch and dinner as well as special occasions, such as weddings and *kenduri* (religious feasts). Although you will find many varieties of rice sold at local markets, the two most commonly used in Malaysian cooking are jasmine and basmati, due to their excellent cooking qualities and fluffy texture, especially when paired with different side dishes. Other types of rice regularly used include brown rice, glutinous rice, black rice and red rice.

Given how abundant rice is, it's no surprise that, beyond being served plain, it also takes centre stage in many beloved sweet and savoury dishes. Rice and rice-based ingredients, such as rice flour and rice noodles, are key to local favourites including *Kuih serabai* (Rice-based pancakes, see page 42), *Apom lenggang* (Crispy sweet crêpes, see page 159), and *Thosai* (Indian savoury pancakes, see page 38). These dishes are typically made by fermenting a batter of rice and rice flour, and are firm favourites among Penangites. Flat rice noodles are another staple, starring in *Char kuey teow* (see page 142), and making tasty appearances in dishes like *Asam laksa* (see page 54) and *Kuey teow th'ng* (flat rice noodle soup, see page 79).

In Penang, street vendors often specialise in one signature rice dish, which they serve throughout the day. One of the most popular is *Nasi kandar* (Mamak-style mixed rice, see page 152) – a favourite for both locals and tourists. Originating from Penang's Indian-Muslim community, *nasi kandar* gets its name from the traditional method of transport used by hawkers, who would carry a pole (*kandar*) across their shoulders with two large containers of rice (*nasi*) hanging at either end. Our go-to spots: Deen's Maju for its delicious mixed curries and NS Nasi Kandar for their legendary *ayam goreng berempah* (spiced fried chicken).

Another iconic Penang rice dish is *Nasi lemak* (see page 28) – it is arguably the most famous of them all. Usually eaten for breakfast, nasi lemak is served with sambal and an array of condiments. The fragrant rice, cooked in coconut milk and pandan leaves, is the perfect way to kickstart a day of exploring. In George Town, we love grabbing a packet from Ali Nasi Lemak or the ever-popular Nasi Lemak Burung Hantu. Other traditional rice dishes worth hunting down include *Nasi kunyit* (Turmeric rice, see page 33) and Chicken rice (see page 62). If you're after something sweet, try *Bubur pulut hitam* (see page 46), a creamy black glutinous rice porridge simmered with coconut milk and sweetened with palm sugar. It's the ultimate comfort dessert.

NASI KUNYIT

TURMERIC RICE

Coloured with turmeric to give it a vibrant yellow colour, *nasi kunyit* is a rice dish often served at special occasions, such as weddings or religious ceremonies. Yellow is the official colour of Malaysian royalty, so serving this yellow rice dish is symbolic of the bride and groom being king and queen for the day.

These days, *nasi kunyit* is commonly served as a satisfying breakfast meal.

SERVES 4

250 g (1¼ cups) glutinous rice
1½ tablespoons tamarind paste
1 teaspoon ground turmeric
banana leaves, for lining the steamer
250 ml (1 cup) coconut cream
pinch of salt
1 teaspoon sugar

To serve

curry of your choice
hard-boiled eggs, halved
Acar awak (Nyonya spicy pickled vegetables, see page 182)

1 Wash the rice until the water runs clear, then tip it into a clean bowl and pour in enough water to cover. Add the tamarind paste and turmeric and stir well, then leave to soak for 1–2 hours.

2 Line a steamer basket with banana leaves. Strain the rice and place in the prepared steamer, spreading it out evenly. Cover and steam for 20–25 minutes until the rice is cooked.

3 Pour the rice into a bowl, keeping the banana leaf lining in the basket, then add the coconut cream and salt and mix until the rice is well coated in the coconut cream.

4 Scoop the coconut rice back in the lined steamer basket and steam for another 10 minutes. Remove from the heat and tip it back into the same bowl. Sprinkle over the sugar and mix well.

5 Serve the turmeric rice with curry, hard-boiled eggs and *acar awak*.

GAT LEBUH CHULIA
சூலியா படித்துறை தெரு
10300 P.PINANG
PEV 4660

BALAI BOMBA

PENANG-STYLE CHEE CHEONG FUN

STEAMED RICE NOODLE ROLLS

Unlike the typical *chee cheong fun* (steamed rice noodle rolls), the Penang-style version uses *hae kor* (shrimp paste) and a sweet-umami sauce that goes well with rice rolls. Readily available from hawker stalls near local markets, food centres and cafes, it's a popular breakfast dish for locals before or after their market trips.

SERVES 4

2 tablespoons vegetable oil

1 tablespoon finely sliced red shallot

1 tablespoon dried shrimp

4 fresh rice rolls

1 teaspoon sesame seeds, toasted

Chee cheong fun sauce

1 tablespoon sriracha sauce

1 tablespoon *hae kor* (shrimp paste)

3 tablespoons hot water

1 tablespoon hoisin sauce

1 tablespoon smooth peanut butter

1 Heat the oil in a frying pan over medium-low heat, add the shallot and cook for 1–2 minutes or until crispy and golden brown. Remove from the pan with a slotted spoon and drain on paper towel. Add the dried shrimp and cook for 1–2 minutes until crispy. Remove and set aside.

2 To make the *chee cheong fun* sauce, place all the ingredients in a jug or bowl and stir until smooth.

3 Steam the rice rolls for a few minutes or according to the packet instructions until heated through. Remove and cut into bite-sized pieces, then arrange on serving plates.

4 Drizzle the sauce over the rolls and garnish with the fried shallot, dried shrimp and sesame seeds.

THOSAI

SAVOURY INDIAN PANCAKES

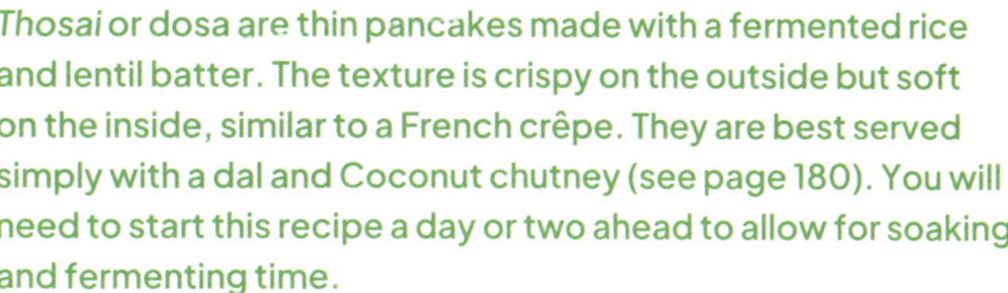

Thosai or dosa are thin pancakes made with a fermented rice and lentil batter. The texture is crispy on the outside but soft on the inside, similar to a French crêpe. They are best served simply with a dal and Coconut chutney (see page 180). You will need to start this recipe a day or two ahead to allow for soaking and fermenting time.

As most Indians in Malaysia are originally from South India, this has become a popular breakfast and brunch dish for Penangites.

MAKES 8

- 200 g (1 cup) *urad dal* (black lentils; see Note)
- 400 g (2 cups) long-grain rice
- 3 tablespoons cooked long-grain rice
- 1 teaspoon salt
- 2½ tablespoons vegetable oil

1 Soak the *urad dal* in a bowl of water for 2 hours. Use your hands to squeeze the dal until the skins split, then drain and rinse a few times to remove all the skins.

2 Place the uncooked rice in a colander and wash until the water runs clear. Tip it into a bowl and mix in the cooked rice and soaked *urad dal*. Pour in enough water to cover the mixture by about 5 cm (2 in) and soak for another 2–4 hours, or overnight if time permits.

3 Drain all the water from the mixture, then transfer to a food processor. Add the salt and 2½ tablespoons water and process to form a smooth but slightly grainy batter. It should be thin enough to lightly coat the back of a spoon. Add a little more water if needed.

4 Pour the batter into a large mixing bowl and cover with plastic wrap or a tea (dish) towel. Leave at room temperature for at least 12 hours to enable the fermentation process. It's ready when the batter is thickened and slightly aerated. Give it a good stir – by now it should thickly coat the back of a spoon.

5 Heat a non-stick frying pan over medium heat. While it warms up, pour the oil into a small bowl. Lightly dip a brush or paper towel into the oil and rub it evenly over the pan.

6 Pour a scant ladleful of batter into the centre of the hot pan. Using the bottom of the ladle, begin to spread the batter in a sweeping circular motion – spreading it out towards the edge of the pan to form a thin pancake. Cook for 1–2 minutes or until the bottom is lightly golden and the edge begins to lift. Loosen the edge with a flat spatula and fold it in half. Cook for another 10–20 seconds, then remove from the pan. Cover to keep warm.

7 Repeat with the remaining batter. If you don't wish to cook it all at once, any left-over batter can be stored in an airtight container in the fridge for up to 3 days. Give it a good stir before cooking.

Note

Urad dal can be purchased from Asian grocery stores or online. If you opt for skinless *urad dal*, soak them for 1 hour and proceed straight to step 2.

BERANGAN PANGGANG

COFFEE-ROASTED CHESTNUTS

Visit Chowrasta Market and you'll find a variety of Penang specialties, such as *tau sar piah* (mung bean paste biscuit), *belacan* (shrimp paste), spices and other popular sweet and savoury snacks.

Just outside the market, there are many stalls selling food and drinks, but the one that really caught our eye was the *berangan panggang* (coffee-roasted chestnut) stall. It's fascinating to watch the hawkers roast the chestnuts with coffee beans – the hint of smokiness from the aromatic coffee works so well with the sweetness of the chestnuts. Wrapped in a newspaper cone, the chestnuts make a welcome snack after a good stroll around the market.

SERVES 4

450 g (1 lb) fresh chestnuts (see Notes)

40 g (1½ oz) butter

240 g (3 cups) dark roasted whole coffee beans

1 Wash and drain the chestnuts, then wipe dry with paper towel. Cut an 'x' into each chestnut to prevent them popping during roasting and set aside.

2 Melt the butter in a large cast-iron Dutch oven over medium heat. Add the chestnuts and stir to coat in the butter, then add the coffee beans and stir for another 1–2 minutes. Cover and roast over medium-low heat, stirring every 5 minutes, for 15–20 minutes, depending on the size of the chestnuts. They will look nice and charred when they're ready. Transfer to a bowl to cool slightly, discarding the coffee beans.

3 When the chestnuts are cool enough to handle, wipe them with paper towel, then peel and enjoy while they are still warm.

Notes

Fresh chestnuts are readily available during the autumn and winter months at Korean or Asian grocery stores, produce markets and some larger greengrocers.

Ensure your kitchen is well ventilated when roasting the chestnuts as they can get quite smoky.

BUAH BERANGAN

KUIH SERABAI

RICE-BASED PANCAKES

There are so many classic *kuihs* (sweet treats) in Malaysia and *kuih serabai* is a popular choice: fluffy and slightly chewy pancakes, usually served with a creamy coconut milk sauce. This is traditionally a breakfast dish for Malays and a popular treat during Ramadhan and *kenduri arwah* (Muslim ritual of praying for the dead). Unfortunately, it's quite hard to find these days as there are only few places in Penang that sell it, though you should be able to buy it in Taman Tun Sardon.

SERVES 4

- 2 tablespoons sugar
- 1 teaspoon instant dry yeast
- 95 g (½ cup) cold cooked long-grain rice
- 125 ml (½ cup) coconut cream
- 1 teaspoon salt, or to taste
- 350 g (2 cups) rice flour
- vegetable oil, for brushing

Sweet coconut milk sauce

- 1 egg
- 500 ml (2 cups) coconut cream
- 1 tablespoon cornflour (cornstarch)
- 1 teaspoon salt
- 1 block (200 g/7 oz) *gula melaka* (palm sugar), cut into small cubes
- 80 g (⅓ cup) soft brown sugar
- 2 pandan leaves, knotted and torn

1 To make the sweet coconut milk sauce, blend the egg, coconut cream, cornflour, salt and 125 ml (½ cup) water until smooth. Pour the mixture into a saucepan and add the palm sugar, brown sugar and pandan leaves. Stir constantly over low heat until all the sugar has dissolved, then let it simmer for about 10 minutes until thickened slightly. You don't want to cook the sauce for too long, otherwise the coconut cream will split. Remove from the heat, pour into a jug and set aside.

2 Combine the sugar, yeast and 125 ml (½ cup) lukewarm water in a mixing bowl. Leave it for 10 minutes or until it becomes frothy.

3 Place the rice, coconut cream and 250 ml (1 cup) water in a blender or a food processor and blend until smooth. Add the salt and rice flour and blend to form a smooth batter.

4 Pour the batter into the bowl with the yeast mixture and fold together using a plastic spatula. Leave to ferment for 2–4 hours.

5 Heat a mini non-stick frying pan (about 12 cm/4¾ in) over medium-low heat and lightly brush with oil. Add a small ladleful of batter, then reduce the heat to low. Cover and cook for 5–10 minutes until the bottom is nicely golden. Flip the *kuih serabai* over and cook for another 2–3 minutes until golden on both sides. Remove and cover to keep warm while you cook the remaining *kuih serabai*.

6 Gently reheat the sauce and serve with the warm *kuih serabai*.

BUBUR PULUT HITAM

BLACK RICE PORRIDGE

With its chewy texture and nutty flavour this creamy porridge is a comforting sweet treat for breakfast. Typically the porridge is eaten just as it is, but fruits like longan, banana and strawberry, and crushed peanuts and toasted coconut flakes can be added for extra flavour and crunch.

SERVES 4

400 g (2 cups) black rice
800 ml (27 fl oz) coconut milk
100 g (3½ oz) soft brown sugar
½ teaspoon salt
2 pandan leaves, knotted and torn

1 Place the black rice in a bowl and pour in enough water to cover. Leave to soak for at least 2 hours, then rinse and drain the rice.

2 Combine the soaked rice and 3 litres (12 cups) water in a saucepan, bring to the boil and cook for 30–35 minutes until the rice is tender but still chewy in texture. Drain and set aside.

3 Place the coconut milk, brown sugar, salt, pandan leaves and 250 ml (1 cup) water in a clean saucepan and stir until the sugar has dissolved. Bring to a simmer, then add the cooked black rice and keep stirring over medium heat until the mixture starts to boil and thicken. Remove from the heat and discard the pandan leaves. Serve as it is, or with fruit and nuts of your choice.

TAU FOO FAH

SOY MILK PUDDING

Tau foo fah is a delicious sweet dish made from fresh soy milk, and it is very common to see hawkers selling it at local markets and *kopitiams* (coffee shops). It can be eaten hot or cold, and you usually have a choice of palm sugar syrup or ginger sugar syrup to finish.

SERVES 4

600 ml (20½ fl oz) Homemade soy milk (see page 187)

½ teaspoon agar agar powder

Palm sugar syrup

100 g (3½ oz) *gula melaka* (palm sugar), shaved

80 g (½ cup) caster (superfine) sugar

2 pandan leaves, knotted

Ginger sugar syrup

200 g (7 oz) caster (superfine) sugar

5 cm (2 in) piece ginger, grated

1 Pour 300 ml (10 fl oz) of the soy milk into a heavy-based saucepan and heat it up over low heat.

2 Meanwhile, dilute the agar agar powder by mixing it with the remaining soy milk.

3 When the soy milk in the pan is quite warm but not boiling, gently pour in the agar agar mixture and stir well to combine. Simmer gently over low heat for about 8 minutes, stirring occasionally, until bubbles start to form on the top. Do not let the soy milk boil.

4 Pour the soy milk mixture into a large container and skim off any bubbles on the surface. Allow the mixture to cool slightly for 15 minutes, then place in the fridge for at least 4 hours or until set.

5 To make the palm sugar syrup, place all the ingredients and 300 ml (10 fl oz) water in a saucepan and cook, stirring regularly, over medium heat until both sugars have dissolved. Set aside to cool completely.

6 For the ginger sugar syrup, place all the ingredients and 300 ml (10 fl oz) water in a saucepan and cook, stirring regularly, over medium heat until the sugar has dissolved. Set aside to cool completely.

7 To serve, use a fine metal spoon to scoop out the chilled *tau foo fah* in thin layers. Divide among serving bowls or glasses and pour your choice of syrup over the top.

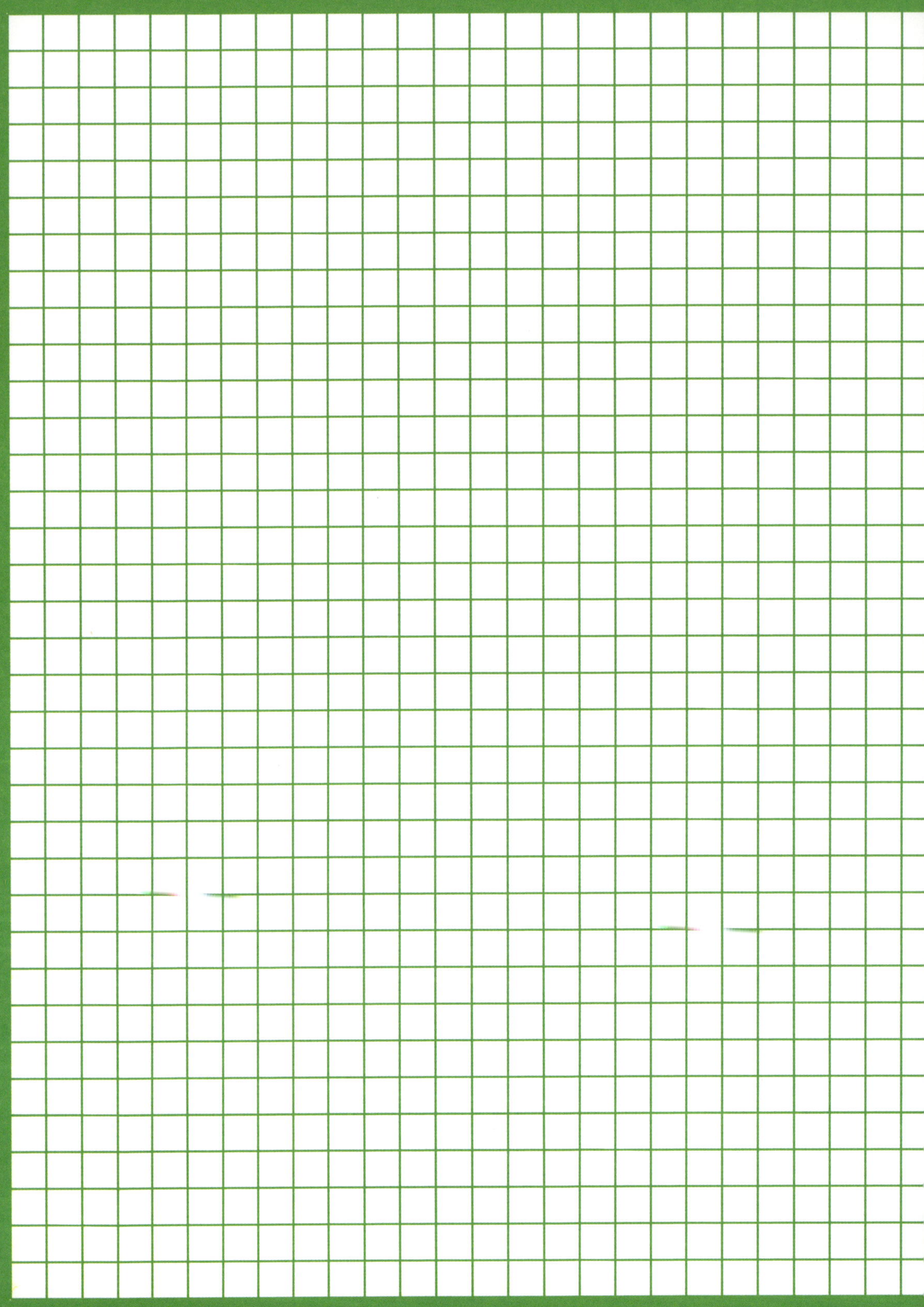

MID

BABAS
rasa asli
kari sejati

Wandering through the sun-drenched streets of George Town, we found ourselves drawn to a well-known *nasi kandar* spot – one of those places where the queue is half the experience. In Penang, lining up for good food is just part of the deal, and a bit of patience goes a long way when you're chasing the best bites. As we edged closer to the counter, the pressure kicked in. Side dishes were swiftly selected (always served with rice, of course), and we had to decide – did we want our *nasi kandar banjir* (flooded) with a perfectly balanced mix of curries, or go for *kuah asing* (curry on the side)? Plates piled high, we shuffled to a small table and gave ourselves a little nod of approval – this was a solid food find!

When it comes to lunch in Malaysia, there are three golden rules: the food has to be cheap, fast and filling. And in Penang, that's exactly what's on offer. Come midday, the streets are alive with hawkers dishing out their signature dishes. From *nasi kandar* (see page 152) to *Pasembur* (a Malaysian-Indian salad, see page 82), and chicken rice to Penang curry mee – there's no shortage of flavour-packed options to satisfy your cravings. Still full from a big breakfast? No worries! Go for something lighter, such as *Kuey teow th'ng* (Flat rice noodle soup, see page 79) or a tangy bowl of *Asam laksa* (see page 54), best enjoyed with an icy *Cendol* (see page 106) on the side.

For the younger crowd, pairing lunch with a specialty coffee has become one of the newer trends in Penang. With sleek, modern interiors tucked inside historic heritage buildings, cafes are booming – serving up fusion dishes that blend local flavours with Western flair.

For the foodies at heart, lunchtime is the perfect window to explore Penang's vibrant food scene and sample some of the best dishes Malaysia has to offer. You'll catch the city at its liveliest at midday, with locals ducking out for a bite or zipping around town on errands. If you're keen on the full tourist experience, hop on a colourful *beca* (trishaw) and let the rider take you *jalan-jalan* (a leisurely ride) through town while you sit back, relax and soak in the sights.

ASAM LAKSA

Laksa is one of the most popular dishes in Malaysia, though there are many regional variations based particularly on the key ingredients in the broth. Penang is one of the major ports along the historic spice trade route, and the invention of *asam laksa* was a cultural and culinary innovation of the Peranakan people brought about by an abundance of tamarind.

In Malay language, *asam laksa* literally means 'sour noodles'. The aromatic tangy fish broth is made with fresh mackerel and tamarind and may be eaten at any time of the day. For truly authentic flavour, top the *asam laksa* with a spoonful of thick sweet shrimp paste (also known as *petis* in Malay or *hae kor* in Hokkien).

SERVES 4

- 80 ml (⅓ cup) vegetable oil
- 2 tablespoons sugar, plus extra if needed
- 80 g (⅓ cup) tamarind paste
- 1 bunch Vietnamese mint
- 2 teaspoons salt, or to taste
- 2 tablespoons fish sauce, or to taste
- 250 g (9 oz) dried laksa noodles or fresh thick round rice noodles
- *hae kor* (shrimp paste), to serve

Laksa broth

- 1 kg (2 lb 3 oz) mackerel, cleaned, scaled and gutted (ask your fishmonger to do this for you)
- 6 slices dried tamarind

Laksa paste

- 20 dried chillies, seeded
- 2 red onions, roughly chopped
- 1 tablespoon toasted *belacan* (shrimp paste; see page 192)
- 1 lemongrass stalk, white part only

Condiments

- 1 long cucumber, julienned
- 2 torch ginger flowers, halved and finely sliced (optional; see Glossary, page 194)
- 1 red onion, finely sliced
- 1 iceberg lettuce, finely sliced
- 4 bird's eye chillies, halved and sliced
- 1 small pineapple, peeled, cored and diced
- 1 bunch mint

1 To make the laksa broth, bring 2 litres (8 cups) water to the boil in a large saucepan. Add the fish and dried tamarind and boil for 10 minutes. Transfer the cooked fish to a bowl and strain the stock.

2 With clean hands, pick the flesh off the fish and discard the bones. Break the fish meat into bite-sized pieces, then return it to the stock and set aside.

3 To make the laksa paste, place all the ingredients in a food processor and process to a fine paste.

4 Heat the oil in a wok over medium heat, add the laksa paste and sauté for 5–7 minutes until it smells aromatic and the oil has separated. Add the sugar and stir for another minute. Pour in the fish stock and add the tamarind paste and Vietnamese mint. Cover and bring to the boil over medium heat. Check the broth and season to taste with salt, fish sauce and sugar.

5 Prepare the laksa noodles according to the packet instructions.

6 To serve, divide the noodles among bowls, pour over the laksa broth and top with the condiments. Serve immediately with a spoonful of *hae kor*.

Note

Dried laksa noodles or fresh thick round rice noodles work best. If you can't find either at your local Asian grocer, udon makes a great substitute thanks to its similar chewy texture.

PERANAKAN CUISINE

The word Peranakan in Malay loosely translates to 'locally born and bred.' Peranakan people are an ethnic group shaped by intercultural marriages between immigrants and locals, resulting in a rich exchange of cultural heritage, ideas and cuisines.

In Penang, there are two well-known Peranakan communities: the Chinese Peranakans and the Jawi Peranakans. The Chinese Peranakans form the larger community in Penang. They are descendants of Hokkien Chinese immigrants and local Malays, many of whom were affluent Malaysian-born merchants who played a key role in driving Penang's economy. The Jawi Peranakans are descendants of the Indian-Malay community. Historically, they were regarded as the elite of Malay society. Today, Peranakans carry a unique blended cultural heritage, and this is especially reflected in their food.

Peranakan cuisine (also known as Nyonya cuisine) in Penang is mostly associated with the Chinese Peranakan community. Early Chinese immigrants, lacking access to familiar ingredients from their homeland, began creating new dishes using local produce. These dishes were developed through a mix of Chinese culinary philosophy and influences from Malay, Thai, Indian, Dutch, Portuguese and English cooking styles.

Today, Peranakan cuisine is considered one of Malaysia's most beloved food cultures, especially in Penang, where careful preparation and special ingredients come together to create traditional dishes, many of which are shared throughout the pages of this book.

NASI ULAM

HERBED RICE

Ulam is a traditional salad made with aromatic fresh herbs, vegetables or fruits that can be eaten raw. Mix the *ulam* with rice, and this simple dish becomes the only accompaniment needed for your favourite curry. Just finish it off with a little Malaysian chilli paste (see page 170) and some fried mackerel.

In Penang, the origin of *nasi ulam* is clear evidence of the strong Malay influence on Peranakan food. In the past, it is said up to a hundred herbs were used when making *nasi ulam*, but these days people simply use what they have.

SERVES 4

- 3 tablespoons dried shrimp
- 1 small piece dried salted fish, deep-fried (optional)
- 2 tablespoons *kerisik* (toasted coconut paste)
- 1 tablespoon toasted *belacan* (shrimp paste; see page 192)
- 740 g (4 cups) cooked rice (see Notes)
- 1.5 cm (½ in) piece turmeric, chopped (optional)
- 2 teaspoons freshly ground black pepper
- 1 teaspoon salt, or to taste
- 1 teaspoon sugar, or to taste

Ulam herbs

- 6 red shallots, finely sliced
- 1 lemongrass stalk, white part only, finely sliced
- 1 torch ginger flower, halved and finely sliced (optional; see Glossary, page 194)
- 3 Vietnamese mint sprigs, leaves picked and finely sliced
- 3 Thai basil sprigs, leaves picked and finely sliced
- 3 mint sprigs, leaves picked and finely sliced
- 4 makrut lime leaves, finely sliced
- 1 turmeric leaf, finely sliced (optional)
- 3–4 betel leaves, finely sliced

1 Soak the dried shrimp in hot water for a few minutes, then pound using a mortar and pestle and toast in a hot frying pan over medium heat until aromatic and lightly browned.

2 Pound and shred the fried salted fish, if using, and set aside, then pound the *kerisik* and *belacan* together and set aside.

3 Place the toasted dried shrimp, shredded salted fish, *kerisik* and *belacan* in a large mixing bowl, add the cooked rice and stir together well. Add the turmeric, if using, pepper and *ulam* herbs and stir again until all the ingredients are well combined. Season with salt and sugar and serve.

Notes

Jasmine, long-grain or basmati rice can be used for this recipe.

Don't worry too much if you don't have all the ingredients for the *ulam* herbs. It can be any combination, based on your taste and availability. If you want to make the herb mix in advance, it will keep in an airtight container in the fridge for up to 3 days. For a simpler dish, just mix the herbs through warm rice and serve.

NASI AYAM

CHICKEN RICE

Chicken rice is a local favourite for Malaysians, and while there are many establishments that sell it, making it at home is not as hard as you might imagine. As with many classic dishes, just about every household has its own unique recipe. The chicken must be cooked to perfection so it's tender and juicy, but it's just as important to get the rice right – perfectly fluffy and scented with the umami flavours of the stock.

SERVES 4

vegetable oil, for deep-frying

Vinegared chilli sauce (see page 174), to serve

1 long cucumber, sliced

Marinated chicken

5 cm (2 in) piece ginger

4 garlic cloves

2 large red onions, roughly chopped

1 × 1.5 kg (3 lb 5 oz) chicken

1 tablespoon oyster sauce

2 tablespoons light soy sauce

1 tablespoon *kecap manis*

2 tablespoons honey

1 tablespoon sesame oil

freshly ground black pepper

Broth

1 litre (4 cups) poaching liquid

1 *sup bunjut* (soup spices; see Note)

1 red shallot, finely sliced

salt and freshly ground black pepper

chopped coriander (cilantro) leaves, to garnish

Scented rice

400 g (2 cups) long-grain rice, washed

500 ml (2 cups) poaching liquid (from the chicken)

1 tablespoon minced ginger

1 teaspoon salt

1 pandan leaf, knotted and torn

Soy dipping sauce

375 ml (1¼ cups) poaching liquid (from the chicken)

3 tablespoons *kecap manis*, or to taste

1 To prepare the marinated chicken, place the ginger, garlic and onion in a blender or food processor and blend to a smooth paste. Massage the paste into the chicken and set aside to marinate for at least 30 minutes.

2 Pour 2 litres (8 cups) water into a stockpot and bring to the boil. Add the chicken, reduce the heat to low and gently poach until the chicken is half-cooked, about 15 minutes. Remove the chicken and place on a wire rack to drain and cool slightly. Cut the chicken into four to eight pieces. Strain the poaching liquid, discarding the solids, and set aside.

3 Combine the sauces, honey, sesame oil and pepper in a bowl. Add the chicken pieces and turn to coat in the marinade, then set aside for 20 minutes.

4 To make the broth, combine all the ingredients in a saucepan and bring to the boil. Check the seasoning and adjust if necessary. Garnish with chopped coriander and set aside.

5 For the scented rice, place all the ingredients in a rice cooker and cook according to the manufacturer's instructions.

6 Shortly before you're ready to eat, heat the oil for deep-frying in a wok or deep frying pan over medium heat until hot and a little smoky. Remove the chicken pieces from the bowl, allowing any excess marinade to drip off. (Reserve the marinade for the dipping sauce.) Deep-fry the chicken in batches for 5–7 minutes until nicely golden and cooked through. Remove and drain on paper towel.

7 Meanwhile, to make the soy dipping sauce, combine the poaching broth, *kecap manis* and reserved marinade in a small saucepan and simmer over low heat for 5 minutes. Adjust the seasoning to taste.

8 To serve, divide the rice among plates, along with little bowls of dipping sauce and vinegared chilli sauce. Add the chicken and arrange the sliced cucumber to the side of the rice. Serve with the broth.

Note

Sup bunjut is a spice mix for soups made with cinnamon, star anise, cloves, coriander seeds, fennel seeds, cumin seeds, cardamom and mustard seeds, wrapped in a muslin bag. You can buy it from Asian grocery stores specialising in Southeast Asian ingredients.

MEE KARI PENANG

PENANG WHITE CURRY LAKSA

This satisfying bowl of noodles is a variation on the classic curry laksa and is a definite crowd-pleaser at lunchtime, especially at food courts. Unlike the conventional curry laksa, the noodles are drenched in a creamy coconut-based broth, then topped with fresh prawns, crispy bean sprouts and a generous scoop of curry paste that you can adjust to suit your preferred level of spice.

SERVES 4

- 125 ml (½ cup) vegetable oil
- 500 g (1 lb 2 oz) fresh noodles (Singapore, chow mein or Hokkien)
- 500 g (1 lb 2 oz) banana prawns (shrimp), peeled and deveined, tails intact
- 180 g (2 cups) bean sprouts

Coconut broth

- 1 litre (4 cups) Prawn stock (see page 186)
- 30 g (1 oz) rock sugar
- 2 lemongrass stalks, white part only, bruised
- 1 tablespoon salt, or to taste
- 120 g (4½ oz) fried tofu puffs, halved
- 400 ml (13½ fl oz) tin coconut milk, or to taste

Curry paste

- 6 garlic cloves
- 12 red shallots, roughly chopped
- 2 tablespoons Malaysian chilli paste (see page 170)
- 2 tablespoons dried shrimp
- ¼ teaspoon ground white pepper
- 1 tablespoon ground coriander
- 2 teaspoons toasted *belacan* (shrimp paste; see page 192)
- 3 tablespoons vegetable oil

1 To make the coconut broth, combine the prawn stock, rock sugar, lemongrass, salt and 1 litre (4 cups) water in a saucepan and bring to the boil over medium heat. Remove from the heat and strain through a fine-mesh sieve into a clean pan, discarding the solids. Set aside.

2 To make the curry paste, place all the ingredients in a blender or food processor and blend to a smooth paste.

3 Heat the oil in a wok or a non-stick frying pan over medium heat. Add the curry paste and stir-fry for 8–10 minutes until aromatic and dark in colour. Remove from the heat and transfer to a condiment bowl.

4 When you are ready to serve, bring the coconut broth back to the boil over medium heat. Add the fried tofu puffs and coconut milk, adjusting the quantity according to how creamy you want the broth to be. Taste and add more salt if needed.

5 Working in separate batches, lightly blanch the noodles, prawns and bean sprouts in a saucepan of boiling water for about 5 seconds each. Transfer to individual serving bowls. Ladle the coconut broth over the top and serve immediately with a generous scoop of curry paste.

ULUNTHU VADAI

BLACK LENTIL FRITTERS

For the Indian community in Malaysia, these crispy doughnut-shaped snacks are traditionally served at weddings and festival celebrations, but these days you can easily find them at hawker stalls around Penang, mostly from afternoon until late evening. They are best paired with kopi 'O' (black coffee) or *teh tarik* (Malaysian-style milk tea).

SERVES 4

- 400 g (2 cups) *urad dal* (black lentils)
- 5 cm (2 in) piece of ginger, finely chopped
- 2 green chillies, finely chopped
- 2 curry leaf sprigs, leaves picked and finely chopped
- 1 red onion, finely diced
- 2 handfuls of coriander (cilantro) leaves, finely chopped
- 1 tablespoon ground cumin
- 2 tablespoons shredded coconut
- 2 teaspoons salt
- 1 teaspoon freshly ground black pepper
- vegetable oil, for deep-frying

1 Soak the *urad dal* in a bowl of water for at least 4 hours, or preferably overnight. Drain, then tip the lentils into a food processor or blender, add 1 tablespoon water and blend until smooth.

2 Transfer the lentil purée to a clean bowl, add the ginger, green chilli, curry leaf, onion, coriander, cumin, shredded coconut, salt and pepper and mix well.

3 Wet your hands and place a small portion (2–3 tablespoons) of the lentil mix in one hand. Shape it into a disc, then make an indent in the centre with your thumb. Repeat with the remaining lentil mixture.

4 Heat the oil for deep-frying in a wok or deep frying pan over medium heat until hot and a little smoky. Working in batches so you don't overcrowd the pan, gently slide a few *vadai* into the pan and cook for 2–3 minutes or until golden brown on both sides and cooked through. Transfer to a plate lined with paper towel to drain off any excess oil. Cover to keep warm while you cook the rest. Eat them just as they are.

PERANAKAN ASAM PEDAS

PERANAKAN-STYLE SPICY TAMARIND FISH

Asam pedas literally means 'sour' (*asam*) and 'spicy' (*pedas*), and this classic dish can be found throughout Malaysia. It is known to be a cultural innovation by the Peranakan people preparing dishes from their homeland using local ingredients and cooking techniques. In Penang, the *asam pedas* has a strong Chinese and Thai influence, giving it a more tangy sweet and sour flavour.

SERVES 4

100 ml (3½ fl oz) vegetable oil

3 lemongrass stalks, white part only, finely sliced

5 Vietnamese mint sprigs, leaves picked

1½ tablespoons tamarind paste

1 torch ginger flower, halved (optional; see Glossary, page 194)

10 small okra

1 small-medium eggplant (aubergine), cut into 5 cm (2 in) chunks

1 tomato, cut into wedges

1 teaspoon salt, or to taste

1 tablespoon sugar, or to taste

500 g (1 lb 2 oz) mackerel fillets (or other fish of choice, such as pomfret, cod or barramundi) skin and bones removed, larger fillets halved

1 roasted candlenut (see page 192), very finely grated with a microplane (optional)

steamed rice, to serve

Chilli paste

1 teaspoon toasted *belacan* (shrimp paste; see page 192)

1 teaspoon ground turmeric

6 dried chillies, soaked in water for 15 minutes

6 long red chillies

4 red shallots, roughly chopped

2½ tablespoons vegetable oil

1 To make the chilli paste, place all the ingredients in a blender or food processer and blitz to a fine paste.

2 Heat the oil in a medium saucepan over medium heat, add the paste and sauté for about 2 minutes until fragrant. Add the lemongrass, Vietnamese mint, tamarind paste, 800 ml (27 fl oz) water and torch ginger flower, if using, and bring to the boil. Add the okra, eggplant and tomato and simmer for another 5 minutes.

3 Season with salt and sugar to taste. Add the mackerel and simmer for 10 minutes. Stir in the grated candlenut, if using, and simmer for another 4–5 minutes to make sure the fish is cooked through. Serve with rice.

WANTAN MEE

WONTON NOODLES

Wontons are small dumplings with a savoury filling, and they are usually boiled in a soup. *Wantan mee* consists of egg noodles served with heaps of wontons, a special black sauce seasoning, choy sum, *char siew* and a bowl of wonton soup on the side.

The Penang take on this dish is slightly different from the Cantonese version, with minced pork in the filling and a topping of pickled chilli for a more satisfying bowl of wonton goodness.

SERVES 4

- 1 bunch choy sum (Chinese flowering cabbage), washed and trimmed
- 400 g (14 oz) fresh wonton/ egg noodles
- 300 g (10½ oz) *char siew* (barbecued pork), finely sliced into bite-sized pieces
- Garlic oil (see page 174), for drizzling
- Dried shrimp sambal (see page 179), to serve (optional)

Wontons

- 150 g (5½ oz) minced (ground) pork
- 150 g (5½ oz) fresh prawn (shrimp) meat, chopped
- 1 teaspoon grated ginger
- 2 teaspoons light soy sauce
- 2 teaspoons oyster sauce
- 1 teaspoon sesame oil
- 1 small egg white
- ¼ teaspoon salt
- ½ teaspoon sugar
- pinch of freshly ground black pepper
- 250 g (9 oz) packet wonton wrappers

Black sauce seasoning

- 2 tablespoons *kecap manis*
- 1 tablespoon light soy sauce
- 1 tablespoon sesame oil
- 1 teaspoon sugar
- 1 teaspoon vegetable oil

1 To make the wontons, place all the ingredients (except the wonton wrappers) in a bowl and mix well. Take one wonton wrapper and place 2 teaspoons of the filling in the centre. Lightly moisten the edges of the wrapper with water and bring the corners together to form a 'money bag'. Repeat with the remaining wrappers and filling, and set aside.

2 To cook the wontons, bring a large saucepan of water to the boil. Add the wontons in batches and cook for 1–2 minutes until cooked through, stirring occasionally so they don't stick to the bottom of the pan. Drain and set aside.

3 Meanwhile, for the black sauce seasoning, combine all the ingredients and 1 tablespoon water in a clean saucepan over low heat. Let it simmer for a minute or so until thickened slightly, then remove from the heat and set aside.

4 Bring a large saucepan of water to the boil and blanch the choy sum for 10–15 seconds. Remove and place in a bowl. Bring the water back to the boil and blanch the noodles for 30 seconds or according to the packet instructions. Drain and place in a separate bowl.

5 Add the black sauce to the noodles and toss to coat and combine.

6 Divide the noodles among bowls and top with the choy sum and *char siew*. Add the wontons and drizzle with garlic oil. If you like it spicy, finish with shrimp sambal, to taste.

CHILLI PAN MEE

CHILLI FLAT NOODLES

Chilli pan mee is a flat noodle dish served with a minced meat sauce, topped with fried anchovies, spring onion, chilli sambal and poached egg, with the option of soup on the side. This satisfying bowl of *chilli pan mee* is a great lunch dish as it is cheap, quick and light, yet filling enough to see you through to the next *minum petang* (tea or coffee break in the evening).

SERVES 4

- 250 ml (1 cup) white vinegar
- 4 eggs, at room temperature
- 500 g (1 lb 2 oz) wheat noodles (from the refrigerated section of Asian grocery stores)
- Dried shrimp sambal (see page 179), to serve
- 15 g (½ cup) dried anchovies
- 3–4 spring onions (scallions), finely chopped
- blanched bok choy (pak choy), to serve

Chilli pan mee sauce

- 300 g (10½ oz) minced (ground) beef or pork, or a combination of both
- 1 tablespoon oyster sauce
- 2 tablespoons light soy sauce
- 2 teaspoons dark soy sauce
- 3 tablespoons vegetable oil
- 2 red shallots, finely chopped
- 2 garlic cloves, finely chopped
- ½ teaspoon ground white pepper
- 1 teaspoon sugar

Fish ball soup

- 1 litre (4 cups) Chicken stock (see page 186)
- 8–12 fish balls (see Notes, page 78)
- salt, to taste
- 1 tablespoon coarsely ground black pepper
- 2 spring onions (scallions), finely chopped

1 To make the *chilli pan mee* sauce, combine the minced meat with the oyster and soy sauces in a bowl. Set aside to marinate. Heat the oil in a medium frying pan over medium heat, add the shallot and garlic and cook for 2 minutes or until golden brown. Add the mince and stir until combined, then add the white pepper, sugar and 3 tablespoons water. Stir again, then simmer, breaking up any large lumps with the back of a wooden spoon, for 5–8 minutes until the sauce has reduced and the meat is cooked through.

2 Pour 4 litres (16 cups) water into a large saucepan, add the vinegar and bring to the boil. Reduce the heat to low. Gently crack one egg at a time into the water and simmer for 2–3 minutes until the whites are set but the yolks are still runny. Lift them out with a slotted spoon and set aside on a plate.

3 Meanwhile, to make the fish ball soup, bring the stock to the boil in a saucepan over medium heat. Add the fish balls and boil for 2–3 minutes, or according to the packet instructions. Season with salt and pepper, then add the spring onion and boil for another minute. Remove from the heat.

4 Blanch the wheat noodles in boiling water according to the packet instructions.

5 Divide the blanched noodles among four bowls and top each with 1 tablespoon sambal, 3 tablespoons *chilli pan mee* sauce and a poached egg. Finish with the dried anchovies, spring onion and blanched bok choy. Serve with the fish ball soup.

NOODLES

A hearty bowl of springy noodles in hot, simmering broth, topped with meat, vegetables and all the good stuff – this is the kind of comfort food Malaysians crave. Like rice, noodles are a staple in Malaysian households and feature heavily in many signature dishes. In Penang especially, you'll find dedicated hawkers who specialise in just one noodle dish that they've been perfecting for years.

Noodles first made their way to Penang via Chinese immigrants who arrived in British Malaya during the 19th century, escaping hardship back home. The largest number came from Fujian province in China, and they brought Hokkien noodles with them in order to create soul-soothing bowls like Hokkien mee.

Cantonese migrants introduced *Wantan mee* (Wonton noodles, see page 72) and *Chee cheong fun* (Steamed rice noodle rolls, see page 36), while the Teochew community brought the much-loved flat rice noodle *kuey teow*. The Hakka, too, added their flair with *pan mee*, a hand-torn noodle dish now popular across Malaysia.

Some noodle dishes were born right here, such as Penang's iconic *Asam laksa* (see page 54). Developed by Peranakan cooks, this version stands apart from the coconut-rich curry laksa found elsewhere. Made with tangy tamarind, flaked mackerel and topped with ingredients like *hae kor* (shrimp paste), it's a beautifully balanced sweet-sour-umami bowl that's unique to Penang.

KUEY TEOW TH'NG

FLAT RICE NOODLE SOUP

In Hokkien '*th'ng*' means 'soup'. Easy to buy from street vendors, this popular lunch dish usually comprises silky smooth flat rice noodles, homemade fish balls, bean sprouts and the hawker's signature clear broth, made from duck, chicken or pork, or a combination of all three.

SERVES 4

600 g (1 lb 5 oz) fresh *kuey teow* (flat rice noodles)
20 fish balls (see Notes)
2 fish cakes (see Notes), finely sliced
200 g (7 oz) bean sprouts
light soy sauce, to taste

Broth

½ duck (about 700 g/1 lb 9 oz)
1 × 1 kg (2 lb 3 oz) chicken
20 g (¾ oz) rock sugar
300 g (10½ oz) *sengkuang* (jicama/yam bean), cut into large chunks
1 piece dried sole, deep-fried and pounded (or 1 tablespoon dried anchovies)
1 teaspoon salt, or to taste
¼ teaspoon freshly ground black pepper, or to taste
1 tablespoon fish sauce, or to taste

To serve

chopped spring onion (scallion) and/or coriander (cilantro) leaves
sliced red chillies
Dried shrimp sambal (see page 179)
Garlic oil (see page 174)

1 To make the broth, bring 5 litres (5¼ qts) water to the boil in a stockpot. Add the duck and cook over medium-low heat for 40–45 minutes until the meat is cooked. Lift out the duck and remove all the meat and skin, then put the duck bones back in the stockpot. Add the chicken and simmer for another 10–15 minutes until cooked. Take the chicken out of the pot and remove the meat and skin, then return the chicken bones to the broth.

2 Add the rock sugar, *sengkuang* and sole and simmer over low heat for another 1–1½ hours to develop the flavours. Season to taste with salt, pepper and fish sauce, then keep warm over very low heat.

3 Shred the duck and chicken meat, discarding the skin, and set aside.

4 Bring a large saucepan of water to the boil. Using a noodle blancher, blanch the noodles in batches for 5–10 seconds until tender. Toss a few times to shake off the water, then divide evenly among serving bowls.

5 Add the fish balls to the boiling water in small batches (up to five at once) and blanch for 10–15 seconds. Toss a few times, then add to the bowls. Repeat with the fish cake slices.

6 Finally, add the bean sprouts and blanch for 3–5 seconds. Toss to shake off the water before transferring to a serving plate. Drizzle with soy sauce to season and set aside.

7 Add the duck and chicken meat to the bowls, then pour over enough broth to cover the noodles, fish balls and fish cake. Finish with the spring onion and/or coriander and sliced chilli, and serve with the blanched bean sprouts, sambal and garlic oil.

Notes

Fish balls are made with a fish paste and are commonly used in fried or soup-based Asian dishes. Look for them in the frozen section of larger supermarkets or your local Asian grocery stores.

Fish cakes are similar to fish balls, and usually come as a thin rectangular cake, though there are many different shapes and flavours available these days.

(S)RM5.00
(M)RM5.50
(L)RM6.50

KARI KAPITAN

NYONYA-STYLE CHICKEN CURRY

The word '*kapitan*' refers to the captains or chiefs during the British colonial era, for whom this dish was usually cooked. Unlike the other curry dishes, this tends to be thicker and less 'soupy', and is wonderfully rich in flavour – thanks to the happy fusion of Malay and Chinese cooking styles.

SERVES 4

125 ml (½ cup) vegetable oil

2.5 cm (1 in) piece toasted *belacan* (shrimp paste; see page 192)

2 tablespoons soft brown sugar

250 ml (1 cup) coconut milk

3 potatoes, peeled and quartered

1 tablespoon tamarind paste

5 makrut lime leaves, finely sliced

1 teaspoon salt, or to taste

Lacy pancakes (see page 24), Turmeric rice (see page 33) or Tomato rice (see page 95), to serve

Marinated chicken

8 chicken drumsticks

1 tablespoon ground turmeric

1 teaspoon salt

1 tablespoon vegetable oil

Spice paste

2 tablespoons Basic chilli paste (see page 171)

2 tablespoons vegetable oil

1 large red onion, peeled and quartered

4 garlic cloves

2.5 cm (1 in) piece ginger

1 tablespoon ground galangal (optional)

2 teaspoons ground turmeric

3 lemongrass stalks, white part only

5 roasted candlenuts (see page 192) (optional)

1 For the marinated chicken, place the drumsticks in a large glass or ceramic bowl, add the turmeric, salt and oil and rub it all over the skin. Cover and marinate for at least 30 minutes, or overnight if time permits.

2 To prepare the spice paste, place all the ingredients in a blender or food processor and blend to a smooth paste. Set aside.

3 Heat the oil in a wok over medium heat. Add the chicken drumsticks in batches and cook for 2–3 minutes each side until golden brown all over, but not yet cooked through. Remove with tongs and place in a bowl lined with paper towel.

4 Reheat the oil in the wok over medium heat. Add the spice paste mix and sauté for about 1 minute. Add the *belacan* and stir-fry for 5 minutes or until aromatic and the oil has separated. Stir in the brown sugar.

5 Add the coconut milk and 125 ml (½ cup) water. Return the chicken pieces to the wok and bring to the boil. Reduce the heat to low and simmer for 30 minutes, stirring occasionally, until the chicken is nearly cooked and the sauce has reduced and thickened.

6 Add the potato, tamarind paste, makrut lime leaves and salt and stir together well. Simmer for another 10 minutes or until the chicken and potato are cooked through. Serve with lacy pancakes or your choice of rice.

PASEMBUR

MALAYSIAN-INDIAN SALAD

Also known as '*rojak Mamak*', this Malaysian-Indian (*Mamak*) salad (*rojak*) is an eclectic mix of prawn fritters, hard-boiled egg, cucumber, *sengkuang* and deep-fried tofu, topped with a thick sauce made with potato and sweet potato. The *pasembur* vendor often stands right beside the *cendol* seller (see page 106), offering the perfect lunch combo for the locals!

SERVES 4

- vegetable oil, for pan-frying
- 250 g (9 oz) firm tofu, sliced in half horizontally
- 5 Prawn fritters (see page 100), each cut into 6 pieces
- 2 hard-boiled eggs, halved
- 2 long cucumbers, julienned
- 1 *sengkuang* (jicama/yam bean), julienned (optional)

Pasembur sauce

- 1 russet potato (about 200 g/7 oz)
- 300 g (10½ oz) sweet potato
- 1 large red onion, roughly chopped
- 2–3 garlic cloves
- 3 tablespoons Basic chilli paste (see page 171)
- 3 tablespoons vegetable oil
- 80 g (⅓ cup) soft brown sugar
- 200 g (7 oz) ground dry-roasted peanuts
- 1 tablespoon tamarind paste
- salt

1 To make the *pasembur* sauce, peel the potato and sweet potato and roughly chop into pieces, then place in a large saucepan of cold water (they should be completely submerged). Bring to the boil over high heat, then reduce the heat to medium and simmer until they are tender enough for a fork or skewer to easily pierce through them. Drain and transfer to a bowl, then mash with a potato masher until smooth. Set aside.

2 Place the onion, garlic and chilli paste in a blender or food processer and blend to a smooth paste.

3 Heat the oil in a wok or a heavy-based saucepan over medium heat. Add the chilli paste and cook for a few minutes until aromatic and the oil has separated. Stir in the brown sugar, then add the mashed potato, ground peanuts, tamarind paste and up to 400 ml (14 fl oz) water and stir to combine. Reduce the heat to low and cook for 15–20 minutes until the sauce has reduced and thickened slightly. Season to taste with salt, then remove from the heat and set aside to cool.

4 Meanwhile, heat a splash of oil in a frying pan over medium heat. Pat the tofu dry and add to the pan, then cook for 3–4 minutes until golden on both sides. Remove and drain on paper towel, then cut each piece into eight bite-sized chunks.

5 Arrange the prawn fritter pieces and deep-fried tofu in shallow serving bowls, along with the hard-boiled egg halves. Ladle over the *pasembur* sauce and top with the julienned cucumber and *sengkuang*, if using. Serve immediately.

Note

Any left-over *pasembur* sauce can be stored in an airtight container in the fridge for up to 5 days, or in the freezer for up to a month.

SAMOSA DAGING

BEEF SAMOSAS

Samosas are a great afternoon snack and our favourites in Penang are definitely from the stalls on Transfer Road and in Little India, which offer delicious fillings and wonderfully crisp pastry. While there are many varieties of samosa, the beef samosa is definitely our go-to as it has a great balance of sweet and savoury flavours.

MAKES 30

- 2 tablespoons plain (all-purpose) flour
- 10 frozen spring roll pastry sheets
- vegetable oil, for deep-frying

Filling

- 3 tablespoons vegetable oil
- 1 large red onion, diced
- 4 garlic cloves, finely chopped
- 2 tablespoons Basic chilli paste (see page 171)
- 25 g (⅓ cup) Malaysian curry powder (for meat and chicken)
- 500 g (1 lb 2 oz) beef (oyster blade or topside), finely sliced
- 3 large potatoes, finely diced
- 2 tablespoons *kecap manis*
- salt

1 To make the filling, heat the oil in a wok or large frying pan over medium heat. Add the onion and garlic and cook until aromatic. Stir in the chilli paste, then add the curry powder, beef and 250 ml (1 cup) water and stir until well combined. Add the potato, then cover and cook for 10–15 minutes until the sauce has reduced, the meat is cooked and the potato is tender. Add the *kecap manis* and season to taste with salt. Remove from the heat and leave to cool completely. The filling should be thick and easy to spoon onto the pastry.

2 Make a little samosa 'glue' by blending the flour and 1 tablespoon water in a bowl. Set aside.

3 Take a sheet of pastry and cut it into three even strips. Place 1 tablespoon of the filling near the bottom of a strip. Lift one corner of pastry from the bottom and lift it over the filling, making a triangle. Continue to fold in this triangle shape all the way to the top of the strip. Brush a little samosa 'glue' on the end and press to seal the pastry. Repeat with the remaining pastry sheets and filling to make 30 samosas.

4 Heat the oil for deep-frying in a wok or deep frying pan over medium heat. Working in small batches, deep-fry the samosas for 3–5 minutes until they are golden brown all over. Remove with a slotted spoon or tongs and drain on paper towel. Serve immediately.

Note

If you don't need the full batch straight away, any left-over filling will keep in an airtight container in the fridge for up to a week, or in the freezer for a month. Alternatively, make up the full batch and freeze some ready to cook another time.

DALCA DAGING

BEEF DAL CURRY

British colonisation of Malaya led to many Indians migrating to Penang. Among the many valuable things they brought with them were the spices used in their traditional recipes. Like many fusion dishes you find in Malaysia, Malaysian-style *dalca* is a good example of Indian and Malay cooking styles coming together. Packed with flavour, this *dalca* is a great accompaniment to *Roti canai* (see page 20), Dal rice (see page 93) and Tomato rice (see page 95).

SERVES 4

125 ml (½ cup) vegetable oil
5 red shallots, finely sliced
2 garlic cloves, finely sliced
1 cinnamon stick
1 star anise
3 cardamom pods
5 cloves
2 curry leaf sprigs, leaves picked
2 tablespoons Malaysian chilli paste (see page 170)
400 g (14 oz) beef (oyster blade or topside), finely sliced
3 potatoes, quartered
1 carrot, sliced diagonally
400 ml (13½ fl oz) tin coconut cream
95 g (½ cup) yellow lentils, soaked and boiled until soft
2 tomatoes, quartered
1 teaspoon tamarind paste
1 tablespoon sugar, or to taste
salt

Curry paste

2 large red onions, roughly chopped
4 garlic cloves
2.5 cm (1 in) piece ginger
3 roasted candlenuts (see page 192) (optional)
2.5 cm (1 in) piece galangal (optional)
3 tablespoons vegetable oil
3 tablespoons Malaysian curry powder (for meat and chicken)

1 To make the curry paste, place the onion, garlic, ginger, candlenuts and galangal, if using, in a blender or food processor, add the oil and blend to a smooth paste. Transfer to a bowl and stir in the curry powder. Set aside.

2 Heat the oil in a wok or frying pan over medium-high heat. Add the shallot, garlic, cinnamon stick, star anise, cardamom pods, cloves and curry leaves and stir-fry for 2–3 minutes until the onion and garlic are lightly golden. Add the chilli paste and stir-fry for another minute.

3 Add the curry paste and stir until aromatic and the oil has separated. Add the beef and toss for 30 seconds, then pour in 500 ml (2 cups) water and add the potato and carrot. Cook, stirring regularly, for 10 minutes or until the potato and carrot are soft. Add the coconut cream, lentils, tomato and tamarind paste. Season to taste with sugar and salt, then give everything a good stir and let it cook for another 5–10 minutes until bubbling. Remove from the heat and serve immediately with roti and rice of your choice.

CURRIES

India's influence on Malaysian cuisine is evident by the country's numerous curries. This influence can be traced back as early as the 1st century AD, but it was the mid-19th century that saw the biggest influx of Indian migration to Malaya when the British brought Indian soldiers and sailors to build docks and work in the new ports. This led to many Indian merchants and *chettiars* (money lenders) flocking to Penang for trade and business opportunities. These migrants brought with them traditional recipes, ingredients and cooking methods from their homeland, sharing and adapting this culinary heritage with the local community, resulting in the Malaysian-Indian cuisine we see today.

The arrival of Indian food in Malaysia came from both the north and south of the country. Northern Indian cuisine boasts a diet rich in meat with less spice due to the presence of ghee and yoghurt. Roti and chapati are the usual accompaniments to these dishes, while rice and *Thosai* (Indian savoury pancakes, see page 38) most commonly accompany South Indian dishes.

Another major influence on Malaysian-style curries comes from the Peranakan community, who incorporated Chinese and Malay cooking styles with Indian flavours to create a whole new genre of curries. In these dishes, local Malay spices were combined to make the signature Malay-style curries we know today such as *Kari kapitan* (Nyonya-style chicken curry, see page 80). These curries are the culmination of Malaysia's multicultural heritage and its geographical position along the colonial spice trade route between Europe and Asia, as well as being one of the key spice producers during the 18th and 19th centuries, with exclusive access to endemic herbs and spices which contributed to the food culture in Penang and Malaysia. Regardless of the myriad styles of curry in Penang, this dish is entrenched in the hearts of all Malaysians.

NASI DALCA

DAL RICE

It's well known that Mamak-style mixed rice (see page 152) is a staple rice dish for Penang locals, but its less-famous sibling, *nasi dalca*, also deserves a spot in the limelight. Originally from northern India, Penang *nasi dalca* is cooked with lentils, ghee and lots of spices. It is usually served with dal and a meat dish, but like any other flavoured rice, you can pair it with just about anything. Try it with Coconut chutney (see page 180), Mamak-style fried chicken (see page 152) and/or Malay-style vegetable medley (see page 185).

SERVES 6

95 g (½ cup) yellow lentils
¼ teaspoon ground turmeric
3 tablespoons ghee
1 onion, finely sliced
1 garlic clove, finely sliced
1 cinnamon stick
1 star anise
2 cardamom pods
2 cloves
2 teaspoons ground cumin
2 teaspoons ground fennel
600 g (3 cups) basmati rice, washed, soaked for 30 minutes, then drained
375 ml (1½ cups) milk
1 pandan leaf, knotted and torn
3 bay leaves
1 teaspoon salt, or to taste

1 Boil the lentils and ground turmeric in a saucepan of water for 15 minutes. Drain, then divide into two equal portions. Set one portion aside. Put the other in a blender, add 375 ml (1½ cups) water and blend until smooth. Transfer to a bowl and set aside.

2 Melt the ghee in a wok or frying pan over medium heat. Add the onion and garlic and cook for a few minutes until golden. Add all the whole spices and stir-fry for 30 seconds, then add the ground cumin, ground fennel and rice and give everything a good stir to combine.

3 Transfer the rice mixture to a rice cooker. Add the blended lentil mixture, then the milk, pandan leaf, bay leaves, salt and 375 ml (1½ cups) water. Stir well, then cook the rice according to the manufacturer's instructions.

4 Fluff up the rice with a fork, then stir in the reserved lentils. Serve immediately with your choice of curry and accompaniments.

Malaysia
enang Shirdi Sai Cen

NASI TOMATO

TOMATO RICE

This specialty rice dish is often served on special occasions, such as Malay wedding feasts; however, in Penang, you can easily find hawkers selling it with Mamak-style mixed rice (see page 152) and *biryani*. *Nasi tomato* is usually served with various accompaniments, including the Malay-style vegetable medley (see page 185), Chicken in sweet and spicy tomato sauce (see page 99) and beef dal curry (see page 88).

SERVES 4

- 1 large red onion, roughly chopped
- 4 garlic cloves
- 2.5 cm (1 in) piece ginger, sliced
- 3 tablespoons ghee or butter
- 1 cinnamon stick
- 1 star anise
- 2 cardamom pods
- 400 g (2 cups) basmati rice, washed, soaked for 30 minutes, then drained
- 1 tablespoon tomato paste (concentrated purée)
- 100 g (¾ cup) frozen baby peas
- 250 ml (1 cup) milk
- 500 ml (2 cups) Chicken stock (see page 186) or water
- 1 pandan leaf, knotted and torn
- 1 teaspoon salt, or to taste
- crispy fried shallots, to garnish

1 Place the onion, garlic and ginger in a blender or a food processor and blend to a smooth paste.

2 Melt the ghee or butter in a wok or frying pan over medium heat, add the paste and cook, stirring, until aromatic. Add the cinnamon stick, star anise and cardamom pods and sauté for 5–10 seconds. Add the rice and stir for another 30 seconds until it is well coated in the buttery spice mixture. Stir in the tomato paste and peas, then transfer the mixture to a rice cooker.

3 Add the milk, stock or water and pandan leaf to the rice cooker pot and stir everything together well. Season to taste with salt, then cook according to the manufacturer's instructions.

4 Fluff up the rice with a fork, garnish with a generous sprinkling of fried shallots and serve.

MoonTree47
PX 1096

Sauce

AYAM MASAK MERAH

CHICKEN IN SWEET AND SPICY TOMATO SAUCE

This classic dish is very popular with the locals, especially in Penang, Kedah and Perlis in the north of Malaysia. The sauce is packed with well-balanced flavours that go really well with the savoury-umami Tomato rice (see page 95) and Malay-style vegetable medley (see page 185).

SERVES 4

125 ml (½ cup) vegetable oil
1 cinnamon stick
1 star anise
2 cardamom pods
2 tablespoons sugar, or to taste
125 ml (½ cup) Malaysian or other hot chilli sauce
2 tablespoons tomato paste (concentrated purée)
125 ml (½ cup) coconut milk
½ teaspoon tamarind paste
100 g (¾ cup) frozen baby peas
1 large red onion, sliced into rings
salt
Tomato rice (see page 95) and Malay-style vegetable medley (see page 185), to serve

Turmeric chicken

1 × 1.8 kg (4 lb) chicken, cut into 8 pieces
2 tablespoons ground turmeric
2 teaspoons salt, or to taste
vegetable oil, for pan-frying

Chilli paste

1 large red onion, roughly chopped
5 garlic cloves
2 tablespoons Malaysian chilli paste (see page 170)
3 tablespoons vegetable oil

1 To make the turmeric chicken, place the chicken in a glass or ceramic bowl, add the turmeric and salt and massage it into the skin. Leave to marinate for at least 15 minutes.

2 Heat the oil in a wok or frying pan over medium heat until hot and a little smoky. Working in batches, gently drop the marinated chicken into the oil and cook for 5 minutes. You want it to be half-cooked and nicely golden. Remove and drain on a plate lined with paper towel. Leave half the oil in the pan.

3 To make the chilli paste, place all the ingredients in a blender or a food processor and blend to a smooth paste.

4 Heat the reserved oil from the chicken over medium heat. Add the chilli paste and cook, stirring, for 2–3 minutes until aromatic and darker in colour. Add the cinnamon stick, star anise and cardamom pods and stir well. Add the sugar, chilli sauce and tomato paste and stir for another 10–15 seconds. Add the half-cooked chicken and mix everything together, then cook for 2–4 minutes until the chicken is cooked through. Stir in the coconut milk, tamarind paste, peas and sliced onion, and season to taste with salt. Serve with the tomato rice and Malay-style vegetable medley.

CUCUR UDANG

PRAWN FRITTERS

I have fond childhood memories of enjoying these fritters as an afternoon snack, usually with a cup of hot black tea. The fritters are often served with either a chilli or peanut dipping sauce but my favourite is definitely Peanut sauce (see page 190) as its sweet-savoury flavour goes really well with the crispy prawns. These are so good on their own, but you will also find them in popular dishes like Malaysian-Indian salad (see page 82) or Mamak-style fried noodles (see page 156).

MAKES 12

- 300 g (2 cups) plain (all-purpose) flour
- ½ teaspoon ground turmeric
- ½ teaspoon salt
- 1 teaspoon sugar
- ½ teaspoon instant dry yeast
- 1 tablespoon *air kapur* (limestone water) (see Note; optional)
- 115 g (4 oz) *kucai* (Chinese chives), trimmed and snipped into 1.5 cm (½ in) lengths
- 1 large red onion, finely sliced
- vegetable oil, for deep-frying
- 12 large banana prawns (shrimp), peeled and deveined, tails removed

1 Combine the flour, turmeric, salt and sugar in a large bowl. Sprinkle over the yeast, add 435 ml (1¾ cups) water and mix well. Stir in the *air kapur*, if using, *kucai* and sliced onion. Allow the batter to rest for at least 30 minutes to yield a crispier fritter.

2 Heat the oil for deep-frying in a wok over medium-high heat until hot and a little smoky.

3 When the oil is ready, dip a stainless-steel spoon into the hot oil and leave for 15–20 seconds, then lift it out and pour about 2 tablespoons of the batter into the spoon. Place one prawn on the batter, then gently lower the spoon into the hot oil. Cook for 1–2 minutes until the batter has firmed up and started to separate from the spoon, then push the fritter off the spoon into the oil to finish cooking over medium heat until golden brown, about 3–4 minutes. Once the fritter is in the oil, start on the next one. Remove the cooked fritters with a slotted spoon and drain on paper towel. Repeat with the remaining batter and prawns. Serve warm with your choice of dipping sauce.

Note

To make limestone water, blend 1 teaspoon limestone paste with 1 tablespoon water. Limestone paste can be easily purchased online or from Asian grocery stores specialising in Southeast Asian ingredients. It is added to the batter to make the fritters super light and crisp, but you can omit it if you are unable to source it.

TAU SAR PIAH

SAVOURY MUNG BEAN BISCUITS

This flaky biscuit is one of the many Penang specialties where sweet and savoury flavours work together in perfect harmony. Traditionally lard is used to make pastry, but because it has a limited shelf life, shortening or ghee is often used instead. The mung beans need to soak overnight so start this recipe a day ahead.

MAKES 12

- 1 egg yolk
- 1½ tablespoons milk
- white sesame seeds, for sprinkling

Mung bean filling

- 60 g (2 oz) split mung beans (without skins)
- 80 ml (⅓ cup) vegetable oil
- 2–3 red shallots, finely sliced
- 1½ tablespoons caster (superfine) sugar
- 1½ tablespoons soft brown sugar
- ½ teaspoon salt

Water dough

- 100 g (⅔ cup) plain (all-purpose) flour
- 1 tablespoon caster (superfine) sugar
- 40 g (1½ oz) vegetable shortening

Shortening dough

- 50 g (⅓ cup) cake flour
- 35 g (1¼ oz) vegetable shortening

1 To make the filling, place the mung beans in a clean bowl and pour over enough water to cover. Seal the bowl with plastic wrap and leave to soak overnight. The next day, drain the beans and rinse several times, then place in a lined steamer basket and steam for about 30 minutes until soft.

2 Meanwhile, heat the oil in a frying pan over medium heat. Add the shallot and fry for 1–2 minutes until golden and crispy. Remove with a slotted spoon, leaving the oil in the pan for later, and drain on paper towel.

3 Tip the beans into a sieve to drain off any excess liquid, then transfer to a food processor or blender. Add the fried shallot and blitz to a smooth paste, adding 1–2 tablespoons of the shallot oil if needed.

4 Reheat the shallot oil in the pan over medium-low heat and stir in the mung bean paste. Add the sugars and salt and cook, stirring, for another 2 minutes. Set aside to cool. Divide the cooled paste into 12 even portions and roll into balls. Store in a container until needed.

5 To prepare the water dough, place the flour and sugar in a bowl, add the shortening and rub it into the flour with your fingertips. Add 1½ tablespoons water and bring the mixture together to form a ball. Knead the dough on a non-stick surface for 1–2 minutes until smooth, then cover with plastic wrap and rest at room temperature for 1 hour.

6 Meanwhile, to make the shortening dough, place the cake flour and shortening in a clean bowl and mix together to form a pliable dough. Cover the dough with plastic wrap and set aside.

7 Divide the shortening dough into 12 equal portions and roll them into small balls. Repeat with the water dough.

8 Take one ball of water dough and use a rolling pin to roll it into a flat disc about 5 mm (⅛ in) thick. Place one ball of shortening dough in the middle, then wrap the water dough around the shortening dough until it is completely covered.

9 Roll the combined dough into a flat oval shape and then roll it up like a Swiss roll. Roll it out again to a flat oval shape, then roll up like a Swiss roll. Roll it out to a flat disc about 5 mm (⅛ in) thick and place one ball of the mung bean filling in the centre. Wrap the pastry around the filling to cover, then flatten it slightly at the bottom. Repeat with the remaining filling and pastry balls.

10 Preheat the oven to 180°C (350°F) and line a baking tray with baking paper.

11 Place the pastries on the prepared tray, seam side down. Make an egg wash by whisking together the egg yolk and milk. Brush the pastries with the egg wash and sprinkle with sesame seeds. Bake for 20 minutes or until the pastries are cooked and golden brown. Allow the pastries to cool on the tray for about 15 minutes before transferring to a wire rack to cool completely. Store the *tau sar piah* in an airtight container at room temperature for up to 3 days.

بسم الله الرحمن الرحيم
JUS BUAH
NOOR MOHAMAD BIN MDABDULLAH
KELAPA MUDA ★ COCONUT SHAKE ★ AIR
NOOR
PADANG KOTA
FAMOUS
COCONUT SHAKE
COCONUT
TEBU

COCONUT SHAKE

Penang enjoys a warm tropical climate all year round; however, the temperature on the island is often higher than the mainland. As coconut is pretty abundant here, this classic coconut drink is a popular choice to quench one's thirst.

SERVES 1

- 250 ml (1 cup) young coconut water
- 135 g (1 cup) ice cubes
- 3 tablespoons sweetened condensed milk
- 1 scoop vanilla ice cream
- shaved coconut meat, to serve

1 Place the coconut water, ice cubes, condensed milk and ice cream in a blender and blend until smooth.

2 Pour into a glass and top with coconut meat.

CENDOL

GREEN JELLY WITH COCONUT MILK AND PALM SUGAR SYRUP

Made with pandan-flavoured jelly, coconut milk and kidney beans in an aromatic palm sugar syrup and served with flaky shaved ice, Penang *cendol* is another Malaysian must-try. Cool and refreshing, it's the perfect treat on a hot sunny day.

SERVES 4

810 g (6 cups) ice cubes, plus extra for iced water

Cendol jelly

4–5 pandan leaves

100 g (3½ oz) *ang kwe* flour (mung bean flour; see Note)

60 g (⅓ cup) rice flour

1 tablespoon tapioca starch

½ teaspoon salt

Palm sugar syrup

200 g (7 oz) *gula melaka* (palm sugar), chopped or shaved

400 g (14 oz) tin red kidney beans, drained and rinsed

Flavoured coconut milk

400 ml (13½ fl oz) tin coconut milk

400 ml (13½ fl oz) milk

1 pandan leaf, knotted and torn

¼ teaspoon salt

Note

Ang kwe flour can be easily purchased online or from Asian grocery stores specialising in Southeast Asian cuisine. If you can find the green variety of *ang kwe* flour, omit the step to make the pandan juice and use plain water instead.

1 To make the *cendol* jelly, blend the pandan leaves with 125 ml (½ cup) water until smooth, then strain the pandan juice into a saucepan. Add the flours, tapioca starch, salt and 500 ml (2 cups) water and mix well. Cook over low heat, stirring constantly, for about 15 minutes until the batter thickens and turns translucent. Remove from the heat and keep stirring to cool it down a little. In the meantime, prepare a bowl of iced water.

2 Working in small batches, add the batter to a potato ricer and squeeze short lengths (about 3 cm) into the ice bath, making sure the jellies are fully submerged. Transfer the *cendol* into a clean container. They will keep in the fridge for up to 4 days.

3 To make the palm sugar syrup, place the *gula melaka* and 500 ml (2 cups) water in a small saucepan and simmer over medium heat until the sugar has completely dissolved. Reduce the heat to low and stir in the red kidney beans. Cook for another 8–10 minutes or until the syrup has reduced and thickened slightly. Pour into a clean jar or jug and set aside to cool completely.

4 To make the flavoured coconut milk, combine all the ingredients in a small saucepan over low heat and bring to a simmer, stirring constantly. Do not let it boil or the coconut milk will split. Remove from the heat and cool completely.

5 Crush the ice cubes in a blender and divide among four small bowls. Add the flavoured coconut milk, palm sugar syrup, red kidney beans and *cendol* jelly, and serve immediately.

PENANG AIS TINGKAP

PENANG WINDOW SHERBET

Tucked away in a little street called Lebuh Tamil, just next to the Chowrasta Market, is a small stall selling *Ais Tingkap*, one of the most famous drinks in Penang.

Also known as 'window sherbet' during the British colonial period, the drink got its name because it was sold from a shop window. More than just a cooling tonic, the drink has many health benefits due to ingredients such as *kembang semangkuk* (malva nut), *getah anggur* (almond gum), coconut water and basil seeds.

SERVES 2

2 young coconuts

ice cubes, to serve

3 tablespoons almond gum, soaked in water for at least 6 hours (optional; see Glossary, page 192)

3 tablespoons malva nut, soaked in water for at least 30 minutes (optional; see Glossary, page 194)

1½ tablespoons edible basil seeds, soaked in water for 3–5 minutes until blooming

Spice syrup

300 g (10½ oz) rock sugar

½ purple dragon fruit (or use 2–3 tablespoons rose syrup)

2 tablespoons dried rose hips, soaked for at least 30 minutes

3 tablespoons freshly grated nutmeg

6 cardamom pods

1 To make the spice syrup, combine all the ingredients and 500 ml (2 cups) water in a saucepan and simmer over medium–low heat for about 30 minutes. Allow to cool, then strain, discarding the solids. The syrup will keep in a clean glass jar or bottle in the fridge for up to 1 week.

2 Crack open the coconuts and pour the water into a jug – you'll need about 600 ml (20½ fl oz). Scrape out the coconut meat and set aside.

3 Drop a few ice cubes into two tall glasses, then add spoonfuls of the almond gum, if using, malva nut, if using, and basil seeds. Pour in enough spice syrup to half-fill each glass, and then top it off with the coconut water. Garnish with coconut meat and serve.

豬腸粥
CHEE CHEONG CHOK
HONDA

SAGO GULA MELAKA

SAGO PUDDING WITH PALM SUGAR SYRUP

Sago gula melaka is a Peranakan dessert that is best enjoyed chilled, especially after a good meal. The ingredients used are very similar to *Cendol* (see page 106), but here cooked sago is used as the base, offering a different flavour and texture. There's plenty of room for both desserts, in our opinion!

SERVES 8

200 g (7 oz) pearl sago

Palm sugar syrup

200 g (7 oz) *gula melaka* (palm sugar), chopped

Flavoured coconut milk

250 ml (1 cup) coconut milk

3 pandan leaves, knotted and torn

¼ teaspoon salt, or to taste

1 Combine the sago and 1.5 litres (6 cups) water in a saucepan over medium heat. Cook, whisking constantly to stop any clumps forming, for 15 minutes or until the sago becomes translucent. Drain, then rinse the sago under cold running water to wash off any excess starch.

2 Spoon the sago into eight small bowls, then place in the fridge for at least 6 hours to set.

3 To make the palm sugar syrup, place the *gula melaka* and 125 ml (½ cup) water in a small saucepan and simmer over medium–low heat until the sugar has completely dissolved. Remove from the heat, transfer to a jar or jug and set aside to cool completely. Store in the fridge until you are ready to serve.

4 To make the flavoured coconut milk, combine all the ingredients in a small saucepan over low heat and bring to a simmer, stirring constantly. Do not let it boil or the coconut milk will split. Remove from the heat and cool completely.

5 Serve the puddings drizzled with palm sugar syrup and flavoured coconut milk.

FRIED TI KUIH

GLUTINOUS RICE CAKE FRITTERS

Fried *ti kuih* is a great snack that most Chinese households make after the Chinese New Year celebration. Slices of left-over *nian gao* (steamed glutinous rice cake) are sandwiched between finely sliced yam and sweet potato to help keep its shape, then coated in a very light batter and fried until crispy. Today, many Penangites enjoy fried *ti kuih* at tea time, available daily from street stalls selling *pisang goreng* (banana fritters) and other snacks.

SERVES 4

- 300 g (10½ oz) *nian gao*, set firm (see below and Note)
- 400 g (14 oz) yam, peeled and cut into 1 cm (½ in) thick slices
- 400 g (14 oz) sweet potato, peeled and cut into 1 cm (½ in) thick slices
- vegetable oil, for deep-frying

Nian gao

- 350 g (12½ oz) sugar
- 430 ml (14½ fl oz) boiling water
- 350 g (2 cups) glutinous rice flour
- banana leaves, for lining

Batter

- 130 g (¾ cup) rice flour
- 90 g (½ cup) glutinous rice flour
- 1 teaspoon ground turmeric
- pinch of salt
- 1 egg

1 To make the *nian gao*, place the sugar in a medium saucepan over medium heat and let it melt without stirring. Add 2 tablespoons of the boiling water and stir until it turns golden, then gradually add the remaining boiling water and stir until the caramel becomes a clear golden syrup. Remove from the heat and set aside to cool slightly.

2 Tip the glutinous rice flour into a bowl, add the cooled sugar syrup and stir until combined.

3 Line two 11 cm (4¼ in) round tins (with a height of about 8 cm/3¼ in) with two or three layers of banana leaves. Place a steamer basket over a saucepan of simmering water. Strain the mixture evenly into the prepared tins, then cover with foil and steam for 2 hours. Remove and allow to cool, then store in an airtight container (see Notes).

4 Slice the cooled *nian gao* into approximately 1 cm (½ in) thick slices, then sandwich each slice between a piece of yam and a piece of sweet potato. Set aside while you prepare the batter.

5 To make the batter, sift the flours, turmeric and salt into a mixing bowl. Add the egg and 220 ml (7½ fl oz) water and whisk until smooth. Add a little more water if needed – the batter should be runny enough to coat the sandwiched *nian gao*.

6 Heat the oil for deep-frying in a wok or deep frying pan over medium heat until hot and a little smoky.

7 Working in batches so you don't overcrowd the pan, dip the sandwiched *nian gao* into the batter, allowing the excess to drain off, then carefully place in the hot oil. Reduce the heat to medium-low and deep-fry until golden brown on both sides, about 10 minutes. Remove and drain on paper towel before serving.

Notes

Nian gao can be stored at room temperature for about a week, but in a tropical climate it is best used within 3 days. However, if you store it in the fridge it can keep for up to 6 months.

If the *nian gao* is soft and sticky, refrigerate it overnight before cutting.

PULUT TAI TAI

BLUE GLUTINOUS RICE CAKES

This popular Nyonya sweet treat is made with fluffy glutinous rice steamed in fragrant coconut milk and served with *kaya* (coconut jam). '*Tai tai*' in Chinese means rich man's wife, and in the olden days it was an elitist dish only served to the wives of rich men. As blue is considered an auspicious colour in Peranakan culture and elegant enough for the *tai tai*, *bunga telang* (butterfly pea flower) is used to naturally colour the dish. You can buy it online or from Asian grocery stores specialising in Southeast Asian ingredients. Of course you can make the dish without the colouring, but then it would simply be *pulut* with *kaya*.

SERVES 4

- 1 tablespoon dried butterfly pea flowers or 1½ teaspoons butterfly pea powder
- 250 ml (1 cup) boiling water
- 500 g (2½ cups) glutinous rice
- 1 teaspoon tamarind paste
- 1 pandan leaf, knotted and torn
- banana leaves, for lining
- 310 ml (1¼ cups) coconut milk
- ¾ teaspoon salt
- vegetable oil, for brushing
- Hainanese *kaya* (see page 191), to serve

1 Place the butterfly pea flowers or powder in a heatproof bowl, add the boiling water and leave to brew for 5 minutes. Strain, reserving the liquid.

2 Wash the rice until the water runs clear, then let it drain. Divide the rice and tamarind paste evenly between two bowls. Pour the butterfly pea flower liquid into one bowl, along with enough water to cover the rice, and stir to combine. For the second bowl, just add enough water to cover the rice. Leave them to soak for 6–8 hours.

3 Set up your steamer over medium–high heat. Add the pandan leaf to the steaming water and bring to the boil. Line your steamer basket with banana leaves (or baking paper) and poke holes in them.

4 Meanwhile, drain both bowls of soaked rice and mix them together. Place the rice in the steamer basket and set the timer for 10 minutes.

5 While the rice is cooking, mix together the coconut milk and salt in a small bowl. When the timer goes off, tip the rice into a bowl and pour over half of the coconut milk. Stir well, then return the rice to the basket and steam for another 10 minutes. Repeat the process with the remaining coconut milk mix and steam for another 10 minutes. By now, the rice should be soft but chewy in texture with an attractive blue and white marbling effect.

6 Line a 20.5 cm (8 in) square cake tin with foil, leaving an overhang at the sides. Lightly brush the lined tin with oil. Add the steamed rice and spread it out evenly. Top with a slightly smaller cake tin (about 17.5 cm/7 in), then place a heavy object (such as a mortar) in the tin. Leave it to press down on the rice for 2–3 hours.

7 Remove the *pulut tai tai* from the tin, cut into cubes and serve with *kaya*.

MUAH CHEE

PEANUT MOCHI

Muah chee is a sweet-savoury snack made with glutinous rice flour that is very similar to Japanese *mochi* (rice cakes). In Penang, it is usually served with fried shallots for texture and added depth of flavour.

SERVES 4

- 1 tablespoon cornflour (cornstarch)
- 120 g (4½ oz) glutinous rice flour
- 1 tablespoon vegetable oil
- ¼ teaspoon salt
- crispy fried shallots, to serve (optional)

Roasted peanut-sesame mix

- 25 g (1 oz) ground dry-roasted peanuts
- 25 g (1 oz) sesame seeds, lightly toasted
- 25 g (1 oz) caster (superfine) sugar

1 To make the roasted peanut-sesame mix, combine all the ingredients and store in an airtight container until needed. It will keep for up to 2 weeks.

2 Place the cornflour, rice flour, oil, salt and 200 ml (7 fl oz) water in a bowl and mix well.

3 Pour the dough into a lined steamer basket and steam for about 15 minutes or until a toothpick poked into the centre comes out clean. Transfer to a bowl.

4 Using a pair of chopsticks or a fork, stir the *muah chee* dough until it is springy in texture. Cut it into bite-sized pieces and toss in the roasted peanut-sesame mix to coat.

5 If you'd like to enhance the sweet-savoury flavour, sprinkle with fried shallots before serving.

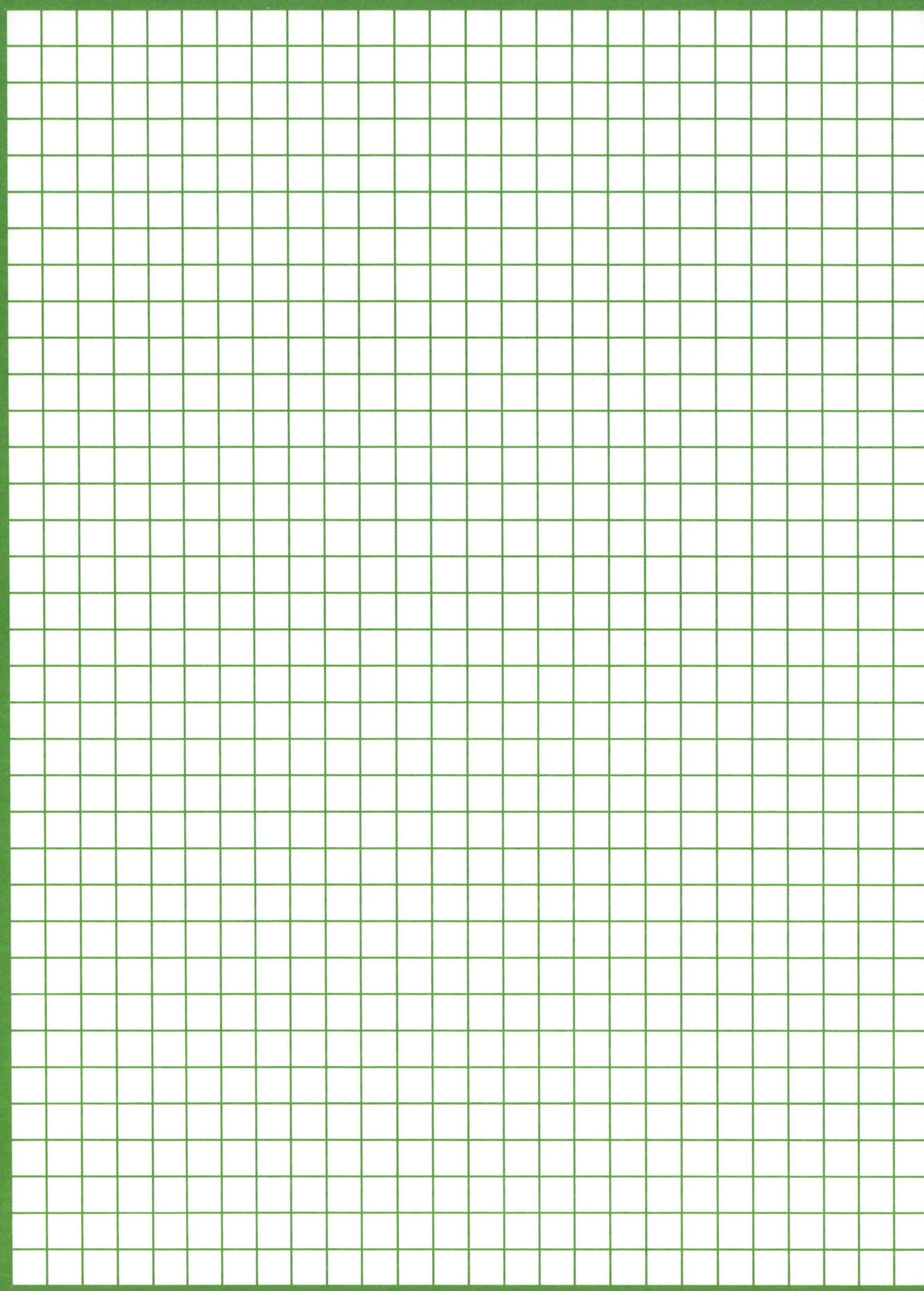

LATE

KEDAI BATU PERMATA ASLI
NAFIL GEMS
Gem Stones With Certificate/ World Bank Notes & Coins Collection
019-472 1188 (Sultan) / 016-411 6184 / 016-470 3838
GEMS
Gem Stones With Certificate
EDISON
PEWARIS ASLI

The culture of *lepak* – hanging out after work – is a favourite pastime for many Malaysians. When the sun sets and the weather cools down, folks love to enjoy dinner, then supper, at open-air food courts, hawker stalls, *pasar malam* (night markets) or restaurants with friends and family. Evening is the perfect time of day for catching up, swapping stories from work or school.

In Penang, the night-time food scene is buzzing, with eateries open till the wee hours – it's like the island never sleeps. From George Town and Gelugor to Bayan Lepas and Balik Pulau, you'll find specialty dishes and drinks from all sorts of cuisines, catering to every kind of diner. Local favourites include *Char kuey teow* (see page 142), grilled seafood, and Belacan fried chicken (see page 146).

Malaysians take supper very seriously, too – no night is complete without a late snack before bedtime. Popular picks like *Lok lok* (see page 150), *Apom lenggang* (crispy sweet crêpes, see page 159), and *Tang yuan* (glutinous rice balls with black sesame filling, see page 166) are said to guarantee a good night's sleep, according to the locals.

Whatever you're craving, Penang's late-night food scene will always have you covered, making the island one of Malaysia's most vibrant and exciting nighttime food destinations.

AYAM MASAK BAWANG

ONION CHICKEN

Ayam masak bawang is simply fried chicken cooked in an onion-based sauce, giving it a sweet-umami flavour that is best paired with warm rice or freshly made roti or chapati. For anyone who has visited Penang, you may recognise the onion sauce as one of the many curries that gives an extra layer of flavour to *Nasi kandar* (Mamak-style mixed rice, see page 152).

SERVES 4

8 chicken drumsticks

2 tablespoons ground turmeric

2 teaspoons salt

250 ml (1 cup) vegetable oil

2 large red onions, finely sliced into rings

1 cinnamon stick

3 cardamom pods

4 cloves

2 star anise

2 garlic cloves, grated

2.5 cm (1 in) piece ginger, grated

2 curry leaf sprigs

1½ tablespoons chilli powder

3 tablespoons Malaysian curry powder (for meat and chicken)

½ teaspoon ground fennel

1 teaspoon ground cumin

½ teaspoon garam masala

2 large red onions, extra, peeled, chopped and blended with 250 ml (1 cup) water

1 pandan leaf, knotted and torn

3 teaspoons oyster sauce

3 teaspoons chilli sauce

2 tablespoons tomato ketchup

1½ tablespoons sugar, or to taste

steamed rice, *Roti canai* (see page 20) or chapatis, to serve

1 Coat the chicken drumsticks in the turmeric and salt.

2 Heat the oil in a large frying pan over medium heat. Add the sliced onion and cook for 1–2 minutes until lightly golden. Remove from the pan and set aside.

3 Add the chicken to the pan and cook for 10 minutes or until they are nicely coloured and nearly cooked through. Remove from the pan.

4 Place the cinnamon stick, cardamom pods, cloves and star anise in the same pan and stir well. Add the garlic and ginger, then the curry leaves, chilli powder and curry powder and stir again. Add the ground spices and stir until it becomes an aromatic paste. Add the blended red onion and pandan leaf and stir until the paste comes to a simmer. Stir in the oyster sauce, chilli sauce and ketchup, and season to taste with sugar and salt.

5 Return the chicken to the pan and stir to coat well in the sauce. Add the fried onion, then let the drumsticks cook over low heat for another 10 minutes. Serve with rice or your choice of roti or chapatis.

INCHE KABIN

NYONYA-STYLE FRIED CHICKEN

This popular Nyonya-style fried chicken was invented long ago by the Hainanese cooks for Peranakan and English households based in Penang during British colonial rule. The chicken is marinated in spices and coconut milk to give more depth of flavour than the typical Malaysian-style fried chicken, and the Worcestershire sauce in the dipping sauce clearly shows the English influence at the time of invention.

SERVES 4

8 chicken drumsticks
vegetable oil, for deep-frying

Spice paste

2 red shallots, roughly chopped
1 teaspoon chilli powder
2 teaspoons ground coriander
½ teaspoon ground cumin
½ teaspoon ground fennel
⅛ teaspoon ground cloves
¼ teaspoon ground cinnamon
½ teaspoon ground turmeric
½ teaspoon freshly ground black pepper
1 teaspoon salt
2 teaspoons sugar
2½ tablespoons coconut milk

Worcestershire dipping sauce

2 teaspoons mustard powder
1½ tablespoons Worcestershire sauce
1 teaspoon sugar
1 teaspoon lime juice
½ teaspoon light soy sauce
1 red chilli, finely sliced

1 To make the spice paste, place all the ingredients in a blender or food processor and blitz to a smooth paste.

2 Place the chicken in a glass or ceramic bowl, add the spice paste and turn to coat well. Cover and marinate in the fridge for at least 3 hours, or overnight if time permits.

3 To make the dipping sauce, whisk together all the ingredients in a bowl.

4 Heat the oil for deep-frying in a wok or heavy-based saucepan over medium heat until hot and a little smoky. Add the marinated chicken, in batches if necessary, and cook for 3–4 minutes or until cooked and lightly golden in colour. Remove and drain on paper towel.

5 When you are ready to serve, reheat the oil over medium-high heat and deep-fry the chicken for another 1–2 minutes until golden brown. Remove and drain on paper towel, then serve immediately with the dipping sauce.

Coca-Cola
Dahaga?

HAINANESE CHICKEN CHOP

This classic comfort dish is an ode to the infamous pork chop, which was very popular at the time of British colonial rule in Malaya. The Hainanese cooks showcased the fusion of 'East meets West' by marinating the chicken in soy sauce to make it more flavourful, then serving it with a sweet, tangy tomato sauce. In Penang, the original Hainanese chicken chop is served at most remaining Hainanese-owned coffee shops, but these days there are many extras that come with it to entice younger patrons.

SERVES 4

4 boneless chicken leg quarters
3 tablespoons rice flour
vegetable oil, for deep-frying
3 russet potatoes, boiled until tender, cut into thick wedges

Marinade

1 tablespoon oyster sauce
1 tablespoon light soy sauce
1 tablespoon sugar
1 teaspoon dark soy sauce
1½ teaspoons salt, or to taste
1 teaspoon freshly ground black pepper

Tangy tomato sauce

80 ml (⅓ cup) vegetable oil
1½ onions, sliced
160 g (5½ oz) tomato ketchup
1 tablespoon Worcestershire sauce
2 tablespoons sugar
1 teaspoon salt, or to taste
2 teaspoons light soy sauce
1 tablespoon cornflour (cornstarch), blended with 100 ml (3½ fl oz) water
2 tomatoes, cut into wedges
80 g (½ cup) frozen peas

1 To make the marinade, combine all the ingredients in a glass or ceramic bowl. Add the chicken leg quarters and turn to coat well, then cover and marinate in the fridge for at least 3 hours, or overnight if time permits. Sprinkle over the rice flour and 2 tablespoons water and mix well.

2 To prepare the tomato sauce, heat the oil in a wok over medium heat, add the onion and sauté for 1 minute or until brown and aromatic. Pour in 625 ml (2½ cups) water and add the ketchup, Worcestershire sauce, sugar, salt and soy sauce and cook for a few minutes until the sauce is simmering and the onion is soft. Add the cornflour blend and stir well, then simmer until the sauce has reduced and thickened slightly. Add the tomato and peas and cook, stirring, for 2 minutes. Remove from the heat.

3 Heat the oil for deep-frying in a wok or heavy-based saucepan over medium heat until hot and a little smoky. Add the marinated chicken and cook for 4–5 minutes or until cooked and golden brown. Remove and drain on paper towel. Cover to keep warm while you cook the wedges.

4 Reheat the oil over medium-high heat, add the potato wedges and cook for 3 minutes or until golden. Remove and drain on paper towel.

5 Arrange the chicken and potato wedges on plates, pour the hot tomato sauce over the chicken and serve.

西刀魚丸
粿條湯
TEOW TH'NG
M 3.50 4.00 5.00 加料另計

325ml

OH CHIEN

FRIED OYSTER OMELETTE

Another popular street-food dish, here pan-fried oysters and chilli are served on a golden omelette with a sweet-spicy chilli sauce for an extra kick. Simple, but so delicious.

SERVES 4

4 large eggs
2 teaspoons fish sauce
pinch of freshly ground black pepper
12 medium oysters, preferably fresh but frozen are fine too
100 ml (3½ fl oz) vegetable oil
2 garlic cloves, finely chopped
1 teaspoon Basic chilli paste (see page 171)
dash of light soy sauce
2 spring onions (scallions), finely sliced
Vinegared chilli sauce (see page 174), to serve

Batter

2 tablespoons tapioca starch
1 tablespoon rice flour
pinch of salt

1 Crack the eggs into a large bowl, add the fish sauce and pepper and whisk everything together. Set aside.

2 To make the batter, place all the ingredients and 125 ml (½ cup) water in a bowl and mix until well combined.

3 Wash the oysters a few times to remove any grit or shell remnants, especially if using fresh oysters.

4 Heat 3 tablespoons oil in a non-stick frying pan over high heat until hot. Give the batter a stir, then pour it into the pan, quickly tilting the pan to spread it evenly over the base to form a thin pancake. Let it cook for 5–7 minutes until it sets and turns golden.

5 Remove one-quarter of the egg mixture and set aside for later. Pour the remaining egg mixture over the pancake and cook for 2 minutes until the edge of the omelette turns slightly brown and the egg is nearly cooked. Make a deep indent in the centre of the egg and add the remaining oil, the garlic and chilli paste and fry for another 1 minute.

6 Add the oysters, soy sauce and spring onion and stir to break up the egg and mix everything together. Pour the reserved egg mixture over the oysters. Quickly flip the omelette over and cook for a few more seconds. Remove from the heat and break up the omelette into large chunks. Transfer to a plate and serve with the vinegared chilli sauce.

KAM HEONG CRAB

GOLDEN FRAGRANT CRAB

Kam heong is a local favourite at most seafood restaurants in Penang, and is often the go-to dish for a special occasion. The words '*kam heong*' literally mean 'golden fragrance', referring to the sweet, spicy and punchy flavours provided by the crab, curry leaves, dried shrimp and sesame oil. All it needs to complete it is a big bowl of fluffy rice!

SERVES 4

- 3 large mud crabs, cleaned and halved (or ask your fishmonger to do this for you)
- 2 tablespoons sesame oil
- 1 teaspoon ground turmeric
- 2 tablespoons cornflour (cornstarch)
- 500 ml (2 cups) vegetable oil
- 2 tablespoons dried shrimp, soaked in water for 10 minutes, drained
- 3 garlic cloves, finely chopped
- 2 red shallots, finely chopped
- 3 bird's eye chillies, seeded and finely sliced
- 2 curry leaf sprigs, leaves stripped
- 2 tablespoons Malaysian curry powder (for fish and seafood)
- 3 tablespoons oyster sauce
- 3 tablespoons *kecap manis*
- 2 teaspoons sugar (optional)
- 1 teaspoon salt
- 1 teaspoon freshly ground black pepper
- steamed rice, to serve

1 Place the crab, sesame oil, turmeric and cornflour in a bowl and turn to coat well.

2 Heat the oil in a wok or large frying pan over medium heat and fry the marinated crab for 5–7 minutes until it begins to turn red. Remove and set aside.

3 Pour half the oil into a jar and reserve for another use, leaving about 250 ml (1 cup) oil in the wok or pan. Heat the oil over medium heat, add the dried shrimp and stir-fry for about 20 seconds until golden. Add the garlic, shallot, chilli and curry leaves and cook for a few minutes until fragrant.

4 Reduce the heat to medium-low. Add the curry powder and cook, stirring, for another minute. Pour in the oyster sauce and *kecap manis* and stir again. Add the sugar (if using), salt, pepper and 80 ml (⅓ cup) water and mix well. Return the fried crab to the pan and toss through the sauce. Simmer for another 3–5 minutes until the crab is cooked through and the sauce has thickened slightly, then serve immediately with rice.

UDANG GORENG TELUR MASIN

SALTED EGG YOLK PRAWNS

This is definitely one of the most popular dishes in Malaysia. Although it's usually made with fresh prawns, variations with chicken, squid or crab can also be found on the menu.

SERVES 2

4 salted duck eggs
1 egg
salt
12 raw tiger prawns (shrimp), peeled and deveined, tails intact
2 tablespoons cornflour (cornstarch) or tapioca flour
3 tablespoons vegetable oil
40 g (1½ oz) butter
2 garlic cloves, finely chopped
10 curry leaves
2 bird's eye chillies, seeded and finely sliced
1 teaspoon sugar
100 ml (3½ fl oz) evaporated milk

1 Submerge the salted duck eggs in a saucepan of water and simmer over medium heat for 10–12 minutes. Drain. Using the tip of a knife, pierce each egg and then slice it in half lengthways. Remove the yolks. (Reserve the white part for rice dishes, such as Mamak-style mixed rice on page 152.) Mash the yolks to a paste and set aside.

2 Lightly beat the whole egg and a pinch of salt in a bowl. Pat the prawns dry and add to the bowl, then turn to coat in the egg. Sprinkle over the cornflour, then mix again until the prawns are evenly coated.

3 Heat the oil in a wok or frying pan over medium heat. Working in batches so you don't overcrowd the pan, add the prawns and cook for 1–2 minutes until golden. Remove and drain on paper towel. Set aside.

4 Add the butter to the wok or pan and let it melt, then sauté the garlic, curry leaves and chilli for a minute or two until fragrant. Add the mashed salted egg yolk and stir until creamy and well combined. Add the sugar and evaporated milk and bring the sauce to the boil.

5 Add the fried prawns, season to taste with salt and continue stirring until all the prawns are covered in the sauce. Serve immediately.

SAMBAL UDANG PETAI

PETAI PRAWN SAMBAL

Also known as 'stink beans', *petai* are widely used in Malaysian dishes due to their versatility and many health benefits. It takes an expert to forage for the long green pods as the *petai* normally hang in clusters at the tips of branches, and in some cases the trees can grow as high as 45 metres (148 ft)! It's easy to source fresh prawns in Penang, and pairing them with *petai* is definitely a local favourite. Frozen *petai* are available from Asian grocery stores specialising in Southeast Asian ingredients.

SERVES 4

- 3 red onions, roughly chopped
- 4 garlic cloves, roughly chopped
- 5 cm (2 in) piece ginger, roughly chopped
- 20 g (¾ oz) toasted *belacan* (shrimp paste; see page 192)
- 150 ml (5 fl oz) vegetable oil
- 1 kg (2 lb 3 oz) banana prawns (shrimp), peeled and deveined, tails intact
- 2 lemongrass stalks, white part only
- 80 g (⅓ cup) Basic chilli paste (see page 171)
- 1 makrut lime leaf, torn once
- 2 tablespoons sugar, plus extra if needed
- 250 g (9 oz) peeled *petai* (stink beans), halved
- 80 ml (⅓ cup) coconut milk
- 1 teaspoon tamarind paste
- salt
- steamed rice, to serve

1 Place the red onion, garlic, ginger, *belacan* and 3 tablespoons oil in a food processor or blender and blitz to form a paste.

2 Heat the remaining oil in a wok over medium heat, add the prawns and stir-fry for 1 minute or until partially cooked. Remove and set aside. Quickly bash the white end of the lemongrass stalks and add to the wok. Leave to infuse the oil for 30 seconds, then add the onion paste and stir-fry for 1 minute or until golden and fragrant.

3 Add the chilli paste and makrut lime leaf and stir-fry for another 5 minutes or until the paste becomes a darker shade of red and the oil has separated. Stir in the sugar and cook for another 30 seconds.

4 Return the prawns to the wok, add the *petai* and stir to combine. Simmer for 5–8 minutes until the prawns are cooked through and the beans are tender. Add the coconut milk and tamarind paste and season with salt and more sugar, if needed. Give it one last stir, then serve immediately with fluffy rice.

CHAR KUEY TEOW

STIR-FRIED FLAT RICE NOODLES

Penang is very well known for its *char kuey teow* and this dish is at the top of everyone's list when they visit. Apart from anything else, it's always so interesting to watch the hawkers prepare it. Some use charcoal fire and others have a gas stove, but every hawker knows that the secret to a good *char kuey teow* is to work fast and cook it in a cast-iron wok over very high heat to give it its distinctive charred flavour or '*wok hei*' (breath of the wok).

SERVES 2, GENEROUSLY

- 500 g (1 lb 2 oz) fresh *kuey teow* (flat rice noodles)
- 80 ml (⅓ cup) vegetable oil
- 4 garlic cloves, minced
- 1 tablespoon Malaysian chilli paste (see page 170)
- 1 *lap cheong* (Chinese sausage), sliced diagonally
- 8–10 large banana prawns (shrimp), peeled and deveined, tails intact
- 2 tablespoons light soy sauce
- 2 tablespoons dark soy sauce
- 1 tablespoon oyster sauce
- 2 eggs (preferably duck eggs if you have them)
- 180 g (2 cups) bean sprouts, washed and drained
- 2 small handfuls of garlic chives, cut into 2.5 cm (1 in) lengths
- banana leaves, to serve (optional)

1 Prepare the rice noodles according to the packet instructions. Loosen the strands so they don't clump together and break when you stir-fry them. Set aside.

2 Heat a wok over high heat until it becomes a bit smoky. Add the oil, immediately followed by the garlic and chilli paste and give it a quick stir. Add the *lap cheong* and stir briefly, then add the prawns and stir with a spatula for 1 minute or just until they turn pink. We don't want them fully cooked yet.

3 Push the ingredients to the side of the wok and add the rice noodles, followed by the soy sauces and the oyster sauce. Stir-fry until some of the noodles get a little charred – this will take less than 1 minute.

4 Push the ingredients to the side of the wok again and crack in the eggs. Let them cook undisturbed for about 20 seconds, then break the yolks and quickly mix everything together. Add the bean sprouts and garlic chives and stir for 30–40 seconds.

5 If you have banana leaves, use them to line two serving plates, then immediately serve the *char kuey teow* straight from the wok.

Note

Make sure you have all of your ingredients prepped and within reach before you start cooking as the process will be super quick.

Certificate of Appreciation

AYAM GORENG BELACAN

BELACAN FRIED CHICKEN

Belacan is an essential ingredient in Peranakan and Malay cuisine. With a history stretching over 200 years, it is believed that *belacan* was originally made in Penang at Kampong Awak, a fishing settlement on the island's north coast.

Although many dishes feature *belacan*, the most famous one among Penangites is *belacan* fried chicken. With its signature flavour and crispness, every bite will leave you wanting more.

SERVES 4

8 chicken wings

vegetable oil, for deep-frying

Malaysian chilli sauce, sweet chilli sauce or any hot sauce you like, to serve (optional)

Marinade

20 g (¾ oz) toasted *belacan* (shrimp paste; see page 192), ground to a powder

2 teaspoons sugar

2 teaspoons oyster sauce

60 g (⅓ cup) rice flour

2 tablespoons plain (all-purpose) flour

1 teaspoon Malaysian curry powder (for chicken and meat)

1 teaspoon freshly ground black pepper

1 teaspoon garlic powder

1 tablespoon shaoxing rice wine

1 To make the marinade, combine all the ingredients in a large bowl.

2 Add the chicken wings and turn to coat well. Cover and marinate in the fridge for at least 2 hours, preferably overnight to help the flavours develop.

3 Shortly before cooking, take the chicken out of the fridge and stir well.

4 Heat the oil for deep-frying in a wok or deep frying pan over medium heat. Add the chicken wings in batches and cook for 3–5 minutes until golden brown and cooked through. Don't overcrowd the pan or the temperature of the oil will drop and the chicken won't crisp up the way we want it to.

5 Remove the chicken with a slotted spoon and drain on a wire rack. Serve immediately on its own or with chilli sauce.

IKAN BAKAR

GRILLED FISH

Seafood is abundant in Penang and if you go to Balik Pulau, you will definitely have the opportunity to enjoy the bounty. One popular dish among locals is *ikan bakar*: whole fish covered in delicious sambal, wrapped in banana leaves and grilled to perfection over a charcoal fire. Served simply with asam dipping sauce and a plate of fluffy rice, it's hard to beat.

SERVES 4

1 teaspoon salt
1 tablespoon sugar
1–2 banana leaves
1 whole fish (such as barramundi or snapper), about 1.3 kg (2 lb 14 oz), cleaned and gutted
5 makrut lime leaves, finely sliced
3 tablespoons Garlic oil (see page 174)
Asam dipping sauce (see page 178) and steamed rice, to serve

Sambal

3 tablespoons Malaysian chilli paste (see page 170)
2 roasted candlenuts (optional; see Glossary, page 192)
2 large red onions, roughly chopped
2 garlic cloves
2 lemongrass stalks, white part only
2.5 cm (1 in) piece ginger

1 To make the sambal, place all the ingredients in a blender or food processor and blend to a smooth paste.

2 Transfer the sambal to a bowl, stir in the salt and sugar and set aside.

3 Preheat the oven to 180°C (350°F) fan-forced. Line a baking tray with a banana leaf. Spoon on 3–4 tablespoons of the sambal and spread it evenly over the leaf. Add the fish and spoon the rest of the sambal over the top. Scatter over the makrut lime leaf and drizzle over the garlic oil.

4 Top the fish with the remaining banana leaf and tuck it under, then bake for 15 minutes. Remove the top banana leaf, then place the fish under a medium-hot grill (broiler) and cook for another 8–10 minutes until the flesh flakes easily when tested with a fork. Serve immediately with the asam dipping sauce and rice.

Note
This recipe makes more sambal than you need. Store the leftovers in an airtight container in the fridge for up to 3 days and serve with any kind of seafood.

LOK LOK

CHINESE-STYLE FONDUE

This Malaysian version of a savoury fondue is pretty similar to Japanese '*oden*' or Korean '*eomuk tang*'. In Cantonese, '*lok*' means to be scalded in hot water, so the name references skewered food dipped in hot soup to cook, served with a range of sauces. In Penang, locals buy their choice of skewers from street vendors for their supper or a late-night snack.

SERVES 6–8

2 litres (8 cups) Chicken stock (see page 186)

Peanut sauce (see page 190), to serve

Vinegared chilli sauce (see page 174), to serve

Spicy dipping sauce

2 long red chillies, roughly chopped

3 bird's eye chillies, roughly chopped

7 red shallots, sliced

2 lemongrass stalks, white part only, sliced

3 garlic cloves, peeled

125 ml (½ cup) vegetable oil

100 ml (3½ fl oz) chilli sauce

1 teaspoon sugar

pinch of salt

Skewer ingredients

300 g (10½ oz) beef, chicken and/or pork fillet, cut into bite-sized pieces

500 g (1 lb 2 oz) medium raw prawns (shrimp), peeled and deveined

350 g (12½ oz) cuttlefish, cleaned and cut into 4 cm (1½ in) squares

250 g (9 oz) fish balls (see Notes, page 79)

200 g (7 oz) crabsticks

10 tofu puffs

10 hard-boiled quail eggs, shelled

250 g (9 oz) button mushrooms, halved

1 x 300 g (10½ oz) packet assorted *yong tau foo* (available from Asian grocery stores; optional)

1 Soak 25–30 bamboo skewers in water for about an hour.

2 Meanwhile, to make the dipping sauce, place the chillies, shallot, lemongrass, garlic and 3 tablespoons of the oil in a blender or mini food processor and blitz to a smooth paste. Heat the remaining oil in a frying pan over medium heat and sauté the paste until fragrant. Add the chilli sauce, sugar, salt and 3–4 tablespoons water and bring the sauce to a simmer. Remove from the heat and set aside.

3 To assemble the skewers, thread the ingredients onto the soaked skewers, using one type of ingredient on each one so they cook evenly. Leave a section of the skewer clear to serve as a handle. If you're not cooking straight away, place the skewers on a tray, cover with plastic wrap and store in the fridge until you are ready to eat.

4 Bring the stock to the boil and keep at a simmer over a portable stove placed in the centre of the table. Dip the skewers into the simmering stock for 1–2 minutes or until cooked to your liking. Serve with the spicy dipping, peanut and vinegared chilli sauces.

NASI KANDAR

MAMAK-STYLE MIXED RICE

Nasi kandar is a traditional dish originating from Penang. The story goes that, during British colonial days, street hawkers would carry baskets or wooden tubs suspended from a yoke on their backs. In Malay, '*nasi*' means rice and '*kandar*' refers to the the pole or yoke that carries the rice and the curries.

Every Penang local has a favourite *nasi kandar* vendor, and a true enthusiast would call for '*kuah campur banjir*', which means flooding the rice with a few types of curry.

This recipe takes a few hours to prepare, but I promise you the results are worth it. Double the quantities to feed a crowd.

SERVES 4

Kuah kari (basic curry)

- 125 ml (½ cup) vegetable oil
- 2 tomatoes, quartered
- 1 carrot, peeled and cut into 5 mm (¼ in) thick slices
- 1 large red onion, sliced
- 4 garlic cloves, sliced
- 2.5 cm (1 in) piece ginger, sliced
- 2 long green chillies, seeded and finely sliced
- 2 curry leaf sprigs, leaves stripped
- 1 cinnamon stick
- 2 cardamom pods
- 2 cloves
- 2 star anise
- 2 tablespoons Malaysian curry powder (for meat and chicken)
- 250 ml (1 cup) coconut milk
- 1 teaspoon tamarind paste
- 2 teaspoons sugar
- salt

Kuah kicap (soy sauce gravy)

- 1 large red onion, roughly chopped
- 4 garlic cloves
- 125 ml (½ cup) vegetable oil
- 2 tablespoons Malaysian chilli paste (see page 170)
- 125 ml (½ cup) *kecap manis*

1 To make the *kuah kari*, heat the oil in a wok or large saucepan over medium heat. Add the tomato and stir-fry for 30 seconds or until the edges are slightly charred. Remove from the wok and place in a bowl. Repeat with the sliced carrot and place in a separate bowl. Add the onion, garlic, ginger, green chilli and curry leaves to the wok and stir-fry until golden. Add the cinnamon stick, cardamom pods, cloves and star anise and stir well, then stir in the curry powder. Add the coconut milk, sliced carrot and 125 ml (½ cup) water. Cook, stirring occasionally, for 5–7 minutes until bubbling. Add the tomato, tamarind paste and sugar and season to taste with salt. Remove from the heat and set aside.

2 To make the *kuah kicap*, place the onion and garlic in a blender or food processor, add 3 tablespoons water and blend to a smooth paste.

3 Heat the oil in a wok or saucepan over medium heat, add the onion paste and stir-fry until aromatic, 1–2 minutes. Add the chilli paste and stir-fry for another 2–3 minutes until the oil has separated. Stir in the *kecap manis* and 3 tablespoons water. Taste and adjust the seasoning if needed – the sauce should be a nice balance of sweet and savoury. Remove from the heat and set aside.

Mamak-style fried chicken

- 4 garlic cloves, minced
- 2.5 cm (1 in) piece ginger, minced
- 1 teaspoon salt
- 4 chicken drumsticks
- 2 tablespoons ground turmeric
- 2 tablespoons Malaysian curry powder (for meat and chicken)
- 2 tablespoons chilli powder
- 1 tablespoon sugar
- vegetable oil, for deep-frying
- 1–2 curry leaf sprigs, leaves stripped
- 3 tablespoons rice flour

Blanched okra

- pinch of salt
- 8 okra

To serve

- steamed rice
- hard-boiled salted duck eggs or regular hen eggs, halved

4 For the fried chicken, combine the garlic, ginger and salt in a glass or ceramic bowl. Add the chicken drumsticks and turn to coat in the garlic mixture, then leave to marinate for 30 minutes. Add the turmeric, curry powder, chilli powder and sugar to the marinated chicken and turn to coat evenly.

5 Heat the oil for deep-frying in a wok or deep frying pan over medium–high heat. Add the curry leaves and rice flour to the chicken and mix well. When the oil is hot and a little smoky, add the chicken and reduce the heat to medium–low. Deep-fry the chicken for 5–7 minutes until cooked through and crispy and golden brown on the outside. Remove the chicken and drain on a wire rack or paper towel.

6 To make the blanched okra, prepare an ice bath. Bring a saucepan of water to the boil over high heat, add a pinch of salt and then the okra and blanch for 5–10 seconds. Transfer to the ice bath to stop the cooking process, then drain well.

7 Spoon some rice into serving bowls and add a small ladleful each of *kuah kari* and *kuah kicap*. Add a chicken drumstick, half an egg and two okra, halved lengthways, and serve immediately.

NASI GORENG CINA

CHINESE-STYLE FRIED RICE

As you have probably gathered, rice is a staple ingredient in Malaysian cuisine, with fried rice featuring at every food court as the go-to dish for locals. It's cheap and works as a stand-alone dish or as an accompaniment to dishes like *Belacan* fried chicken (see page 146), Fried oyster omelette (see page 134) and Salted egg yolk prawns (see page 138).

If you are cooking fried rice at home you'll find endless variations using different ingredients, but this version is probably one of the simplest and best loved. Even better, you can use left-over rice from a previous meal to make this delicious and satisfying dinner.

SERVES 4

- 3 tablespoons vegetable oil
- 3 garlic cloves, finely chopped
- 2 red shallots, finely sliced
- 2 long red chillies, seeded and finely sliced
- 12 banana prawns (shrimp), peeled and deveined, tails intact
- 3 eggs
- 70 g (½ cup) frozen mixed vegetables, thawed
- 2 tablespoons oyster sauce
- 1 teaspoon fish sauce
- 740 g (4 cups) left-over cooked long-grain or basmati rice, chilled overnight
- 2 tablespoons sesame oil
- salt and freshly ground black pepper
- Malaysian chilli paste (see page 170), to serve (optional)

1 Heat the oil in a wok or a non-stick frying pan over medium heat. Add the garlic, shallot and chilli and cook for 1–2 minutes until aromatic. Add the prawns and cook for 1 minute.

2 Push the sautéed ingredients to the edge of the wok and crack in the eggs. Let them cook for 30 seconds or so, then break up the eggs using a spatula.

3 Add the frozen vegetables and stir well, then pour in the oyster sauce and fish sauce and stir to combine. Add the rice and toss everything together.

4 Add the sesame oil and season to taste with salt and pepper. Continue stirring until the rice becomes toasty, then serve immediately with Malaysian chilli paste if you like a little extra 'kick'.

MEE GORENG MAMAK

MAMAK-STYLE FRIED NOODLES

Unlike regular fried noodles, this delicious dish is packed with sweet and spicy flavours along with a hint of nuttiness from the special *mee goreng Mamak* paste. In Penang, our favourite vendors are the ones in Tanjung Bungah and Jelutong, where the hawkers stir-fry the noodles over charcoal in less than 5 minutes, adding a wonderful charred flavour to an already great plate of noodles.

SERVES 4

100 ml (3½ fl oz) vegetable oil
250 g (9 oz) firm tofu, sliced in half horizontally
3 garlic cloves, finely chopped
2 red shallots, finely sliced
2 Prawn fritters (see page 100), cut into bite-sized pieces
2 small potatoes, peeled, boiled and cut into bite-sized pieces
2 small tomatoes, cut into bite-sized pieces
300 g (10½ oz) yellow noodles (Singapore, chow mein or Hokkien noodles), blanched according to the packet instructions
4 small eggs
90 g (1 cup) bean sprouts

1 To make the *mee goreng Mamak* paste, heat the oil in a wok over medium heat and fry the yellow lentils for about 1 minute. Add the dried shrimp and stir until golden brown. Scoop out the lentil and dried shrimp mix using a fine-mesh sieve and reserve the frying oil.

2 Place the fried lentil mixture, chilli paste and 3–4 tablespoons of the frying oil in a blender or food processor and blend to a smooth paste.

3 Heat the remaining frying oil in the wok over medium heat and stir-fry the paste for 3–4 minutes until aromatic and the oil has separated. Stir in the sugar, then add the ground peanuts, tamarind paste and 500 ml (2 cups) water and mix together well. Season to taste with salt, then simmer for 8–10 minutes until the sauce has reduced and thickened, and the oil has separated. Remove from the heat and leave to cool to room temperature.

4 Heat 2 tablespoons of the oil in a frying pan over medium heat. Pat the tofu dry and add to the pan, then cook for 3–4 minutes until golden on both sides. Remove and drain on paper towel, then cut each piece into bite-sized chunks.

Note
Left-over *mee goreng Mamak* paste can be stored in an airtight container in the fridge for up to 5 days or in the freezer for 1 month. Delicious tossed through your favourite noodles.

Mee goreng Mamak paste

- 125 ml (½ cup) vegetable oil
- 1 tablespoon yellow lentils
- 80 g (1 cup) dried shrimp, soaked in water for 10 minutes, drained
- 2½ tablespoons Malaysian chilli paste (see page 170)
- 3–4 tablespoons sugar
- 125 g (4½ oz) ground dry-roasted peanuts
- 1 tablespoon tamarind paste
- salt

Garnishes

- 1 cos (romaine) lettuce, shredded
- 2 long red chillies, sliced
- crispy fried shallots
- 2 limes, quartered

5 Heat the remaining oil in a wok or a non-stick frying pan over medium heat. Add the garlic and shallot and cook until golden and fragrant. Add the tofu, prawn fritter pieces, potato and tomato and stir-fry for about 30 seconds until combined.

6 Add 3–4 tablespoons of the *mee goreng Mamak* paste and stir constantly for another 30 seconds. Add the blanched noodles and toss through. Make a well in the middle of the noodle mixture and crack in the eggs. Let them cook for 30 seconds or so, then break up the eggs using a spatula. Stir again for another 30 seconds to mix everything together. Finally, toss through the bean sprouts.

7 Divide the fried noodles among plates and garnish with the lettuce, chilli, crispy fried shallots and lime quarters. Serve immediately.

APOM LENGGANG

CRISPY SWEET CRÊPES

If you walk along the night hawker area in Chulia Street, George Town, you will find a stall selling soft yet crispy *apom*, which is the perfect after-dinner snack. Originally, *apom* makers used charcoal and a clay pot to make these treats, but these days a simpler, more portable set-up is called for. With four mini woks lined up, you can't fail to be impressed at how quickly the seller makes the *apom* while taking orders at the same time.

SERVES 4

- 140 g (¾ cup) cold cooked long-grain rice
- 265 g (1½ cups) rice flour
- 75 g (½ cup) plain (all-purpose) flour
- 115 g (½ cup) caster (superfine) sugar
- 1 teaspoon instant dry yeast
- 250 ml (1 cup) coconut milk
- 1 egg
- pinch of salt
- vegetable oil, for brushing

1 Place the rice and 375 ml (1½ cups) water in a blender and blend until smooth and well combined.

2 Tip the rice mixture into a clean bowl, add the flours, sugar, yeast, coconut milk, egg and salt and mix together well. Set aside to rest at room temperature for 1 hour. Alternatively, the batter can be made in advance and left to rest in the fridge overnight.

3 Mix the batter again to remove any lumps. You can strain it if needed to achieve a really smooth batter.

4 Heat a small non-stick frying pan over medium heat and brush with a little oil. Scoop in a small ladleful of batter and tilt the pan to spread it evenly into a thin layer, like you are making a crêpe. Cook for 2–3 minutes until the base is crisp and golden, then slide the *apom* onto a plate and gently fold it in half. Cover to keep warm. Repeat with the remaining batter, then serve immediately.

雲吞麵
3.30 (SMALL)
4.50 (BIG)

PENANG

LONGAN TONG SUI

LONGAN SWEET SOUP

It is a ritual for Penangites to have a sweet dessert or snack after dinner to end a good day, and *tong sui* is very popular with the locals. This Cantonese specialty, which literally means 'sugar water', is a sweet soup made with either water or coconut milk. These days, you'll find various flavour combinations on offer (such as black sesame, sweet potato and mango sago) and the soup can be served hot or cold, depending on your preference.

Some of the ingredients may be unfamiliar, but you can easily buy snow fungus, dried longan, red dates, ginkgo nuts and pandan leaves online or at Asian grocery stores. You can customise your dish by substituting or adding goji berries, papaya, pears and apples, but the main stars should be the dried longan and red dates.

SERVES 4

- 5 g (¼ oz) snow fungus
- 50 g (1¾ oz) dried longan
- 20 g (¾ oz) red dates
- 20 g (¾ oz) ginkgo nuts
- 50 g (1¾ oz) sugar, or to taste
- 2 pandan leaves, knotted and torn

1 Soften the snow fungus by soaking it in water for 20 minutes. Using kitchen scissors, trim off the yellowish part at the bottom and then cut the fungus into smaller pieces. Set aside.

2 Rinse the longan, red dates and ginkgo nuts under running water and set aside.

3 Pour 1 litre (4 cups) water into a saucepan and bring to the boil. Reduce the heat to medium and add the snow fungus, longan, red dates, ginkgo nuts, sugar and pandan leaves, then gently simmer over low heat for about 45 minutes until everything is cooked through. Top up the water if needed and adjust the sweetness to suit your taste. Serve warm or chilled. Any leftovers will keep in an airtight container in the fridge for up to 3 days.

DESSERTS

Malaysia's multicultural heritage really shines through in the variety of desserts enjoyed across the country. And Penang, with its own distinct twist on many sweet treats, is no exception. Unlike Western-style desserts, Malaysian desserts often look quite simple on the outside, but once you dig in, there's an explosion of flavour and textures to surprise you.

For Malaysians, desserts are eaten any time of the day; hot or cold, there are plenty of options to choose from, so you're truly spoilt for choice. Some of Penang's most loved desserts include *Tau foo fah* (soy milk pudding, see page 48), string hoppers (see page 23), usually served with coconut and brown sugar, and *Kuih serabai* (rice-based pancakes, see page 42) paired with a gooey, sweet coconut milk sauce. Traditionally, these are enjoyed before lunch, so if you're in Penang, swing by a local morning market or a breakfast-style food court for a proper treat.

In the afternoon, when the weather's hot and sunny, locals often cool down with a bowl of *Cendol* (see page 106), a Penang specialty made with finely shaved ice and topped with condiments like *cendol* jelly, coconut milk, brown sugar syrup and kidney beans. Super refreshing and full of flavour.

Peranakan desserts are another highlight – they are colourful, rich in flavour, and Chinese in influence. Many carry symbolic meaning for the communities who make them. Popular picks in Penang include sago pudding (see page 111) and *Pulut tai tai* (blue glutinous rice cakes, see page 116), both perfect as a post-meal indulgence.

But if you want to indulge like a true local, save some room for dessert from the night food markets, when the weather cools down and the dessert stalls come alive. Here you'll find *Tong sui* (longan sweet soup, see page 162) and *Tang yuan* (glutinous rice balls with black sesame filling, see page 166), both served with a variety of fillings, flavours and toppings that'll make choosing only one nearly impossible. If you're after something lighter, you can't go wrong with *Apom lenggang* (see page 159), perfectly crisp sweet pancakes that hit the spot.

White Coffee
BUAH SALAK

TANG YUAN

GLUTINOUS RICE BALLS WITH BLACK SESAME FILLING

This is another favourite for a late-night dessert. Traditionally eaten as a symbol of unity and often served during the Winter Solstice Festival, *tang yuan* are now enjoyed daily by locals when the weather is slightly cooler at night. The combination of soft, chewy glutinous rice balls, black sesame filling and ginger syrup give a great balance of sweetness, nuttiness and enough 'heat' to finish your day with a bang.

MAKES 24

- 250 g (9 oz) glutinous rice flour, plus 50 g (1¾ oz) extra for kneading
- 125 ml (½ cup) boiling water
- 125 ml (½ cup) chilled water

Black sesame filling

- 3 tablespoons black sesame seeds (see Notes)
- 3 tablespoons caster (superfine) sugar
- 3 tablespoons coconut oil or melted butter

Ginger syrup

- 75 g (2½ oz) ginger, cut into chunks
- 1 pandan leaf, knotted and torn
- 115 g (½ cup) caster (superfine) sugar
- ½ teaspoon osmanthus (optional; see Notes)

1 To make the black sesame filling, toast the black sesame seeds in a small frying pan over medium-low heat until fragrant (don't let them burn). It's worth covering the pan with a lid as the seeds will start popping as they heat up. Tip the toasted seeds into a bowl and let them cool.

2 Finely grind the cooled seeds in a food processor. Add the sugar and coconut oil or butter, then pulse for 10 seconds until well combined. Transfer to a bowl and place in the fridge for at least 30 minutes to firm up. This will make it easier to handle later.

3 Place the glutinous rice flour in a large bowl and make a well in the centre. Pour the boiling water into the well and stir with a spoon or spatula. (Adding hot water will give the rice balls the chewy texture you're after.) Add the chilled water, then knead, slowly adding the extra flour, until the dough is smooth and no longer sticky, about 10 minutes. Divide the dough into 24 portions and roll each one into a ball, then cover with a tea (dish) towel so they don't dry out.

4 Check the black sesame filling – it should be firm but pliable. Roll the filling into 24 small balls.

5 Working with one ball of dough at a time, flatten it into a circle about 5 cm (2 in) in diameter and place a ball of filling in the centre. Wrap the dough around the filling, making sure it is completely enclosed, then roll it into a smooth ball. Repeat with the remaining dough and filling, then cover and set aside.

6 To make the ginger syrup, pour 625 ml (2½ cups) water into a saucepan and bring to the boil. Add the ginger and pandan leaf and bring back to the boil. Reduce the heat to low, then cover and simmer for 10–15 minutes to infuse the ginger and pandan flavours into the water. Add the sugar and osmanthus, if using, and let it boil over medium heat for another 5 minutes or until the sugar has dissolved. Reduce the heat to low and simmer gently for another 10 minutes or so until the liquid has reduced and thickened slightly. Remove and discard the ginger and pandan leaf and set aside the syrup.

Notes

When toasting the black sesame seeds, you can add 1 teaspoon of white sesame seeds to help keep an eye on the colour. Take them off the heat as soon as the white seeds are golden.

Osmanthus is a syrup infused with the osmanthus flower. You can buy it from Asian grocery stores or Chinese medical practitioners. If you can't find it, don't worry – the syrup will still taste great without it.

If you don't want to serve all the *tang yuan* at once, place the uncooked dough balls, well spaced so they aren't touching, on a tray lined with baking paper. Freeze for 15 minutes, then pop them in a freezer bag or container.

They'll keep for up to 3 months in the freezer. When you're ready to cook them, add the frozen *tang yuan* to a saucepan of boiling water for 5–7 minutes until heated through. Serve with the ginger syrup.

7 Bring a large saucepan of water to the boil. Working in batches so you don't overcrowd the pan, add the glutinous rice balls and cook for 3–5 minutes, stirring occasionally to prevent them from sticking together. They are ready when they float to the surface. Lift out the cooked rice balls and put them straight into a bowl of cold water to stop the cooking process. This helps make them nice and chewy.

8 Place all the cooked rice balls in the warm ginger syrup and serve immediately. If you prefer a cold *tang yuan*, let it chill in the fridge for a while first.

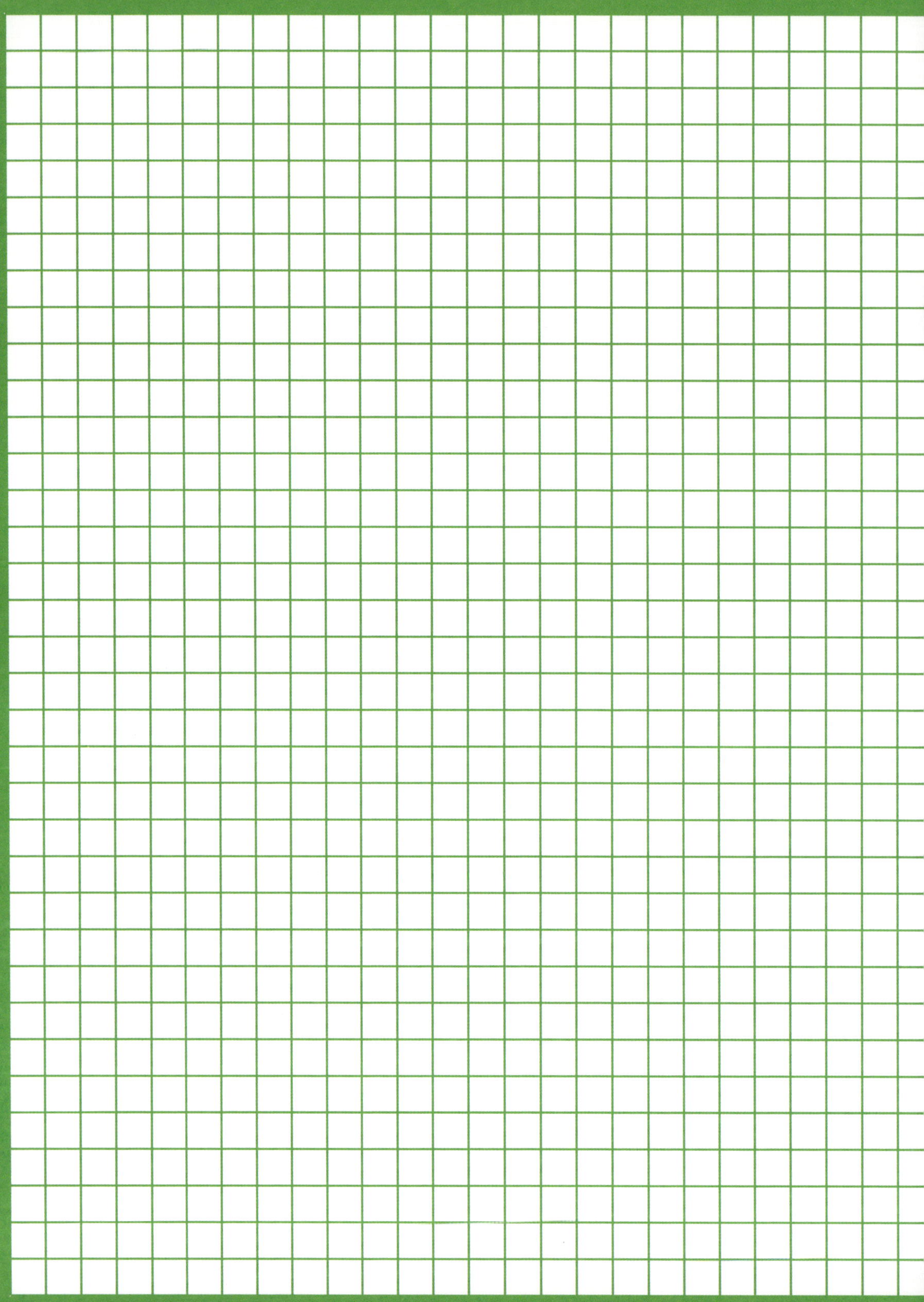

BASICS

SAMBAL BELACAN

MALAYSIAN CHILLI PASTE

Sambal belacan is a basic condiment in most Malaysian households and is a great addition to rice or noodle dishes if you like a bit of zing!

MAKES ABOUT 150 ML (5 FL OZ)

5 long red chillies

5 bird's eye chillies

1 tablespoon toasted *belacan* (shrimp paste; see page 192)

1 teaspoon sugar

pinch of salt

juice of ½ lime

1 Using a mortar and pestle, pound all the chillies to make a coarse paste.

2 Add the *belacan*, sugar and salt and pound for another minute. Add the lime juice and mix well.

3 Store in a clean jar in the fridge for up to 2 weeks.

Note

If you are using a small chopper or blender, add all the ingredients except the lime juice and blend to a smooth paste. Then stir in the lime juice.

BASIC CHILLI PASTE

A good chilli paste is one of the most important ingredients in Malaysian cooking, especially if you're making stir-fried noodles or sambal-based dishes. It's generally better to use the curlier type of dried chillies as they have been dried for longer, making them significantly less spicy. This results in a nice dark red paste with a mellow flavour.

MAKES ABOUT 750 G (3 CUPS)

- 500 g (1 lb 2 oz) dried chillies
- 3 garlic bulbs, cloves separated and peeled
- 250 ml (1 cup) vegetable oil
- 2 tablespoons salt

1 Cut the dried chillies in half lengthways and remove as many seeds as possible, then soak the chillies in water for 15 minutes.

2 Drain and rinse the chillies, then place in a saucepan with the garlic and enough water to cover them. Bring to the boil, then drain and set aside to cool.

3 Using a food processor or a blender (and working in batches if necessary), process the chilli and garlic mixture with the oil and salt to a smooth paste. Transfer to one large container or a few smaller ones, then cover and store in the fridge for up to 1 month.

BELACAN

Belacan, or fermented shrimp paste, is an essential ingredient used in Malaysian cooking, particularly in Malay and Peranakan cuisines. This salty-umami condiment is made from krill (tiny shrimp-like crustaceans) that are usually salted, sundried and then fermented. This fermentation enables the *belacan* to naturally develop its flavour and ensure that it has a long shelf life. According to locals, the more pungent the smell of the *belacan*, the better the taste, and it's safe to say that Penang makes some of the best *belacan* in Malaysia.

It is thought that the first *belacan* was manufactured in Malacca about 200 years ago, earning it the nickname 'Malacca cheese'. However, other sources suggest that it was originally made in Penang at a fishermen's village called Kampung Awak, located on the island's north coast. Regardless of its origin, it remains an essential condiment in all Malaysian households, where it is used heavily in cooking as a flavour enhancer.

Belacan is a signature ingredient in many sambals. It is also used in marinades for fried chicken, such as *Belacan* fried chicken (see page 146), adding the depth of flavour and salty-umami taste found in so many Malaysian dishes. *Belacan* is never eaten raw, and toasting it over flames or baking it in the oven helps impart its unique flavour. One of the best ways to use toasted *belacan* is to make *Sambal belacan* (see page 170). This hot and spicy condiment is made by pounding the shrimp paste with chilli, lime, salt and sugar using a mortar and pestle. It is then served as an accompaniment with any number of local dishes.

SAMBAL CILI CUKA

VINEGARED CHILLI SAUCE

This vinegared chilli sauce is a must-have condiment for adding extra 'oomph' to many of your favourite dishes. Serve it with Chicken rice (see page 62) or as a dipping sauce for Chinese-style fondue (see page 150). It's super easy to make and you can adjust the level of spice and sweetness to suit your personal preference.

MAKES ABOUT 500 ML (2 CUPS)

- 10 long red chillies, roughly chopped
- 125 ml (½ cup) Chicken stock (see page 186)
- 2 tablespoons sugar
- 80 ml (⅓ cup) apple cider vinegar
- 1 teaspoon salt

1 Place all the ingredients in a blender or food processor and blend to a smooth paste. Taste and adjust according to your preference. The spiciness, sweetness and acidity should be balanced.

2 Transfer to an airtight container or a glass jar and store in the fridge for up to 1 week.

Note

If you don't have any chicken stock, just replace it with water or any other stock you have at hand.

GARLIC OIL

Garlic is another star ingredient in Malaysian cooking. Use this pungent, versatile oil to top noodle dishes, drizzle over flat noodle soups or toss through stir-fried vegetables – it's good for any savoury dish that could do with a little extra 'oomph'.

MAKES ABOUT 250 ML (1 CUP)

- 180 ml (¾ cup) vegetable oil or olive oil
- 2 garlic bulbs (about 20 cloves), peeled and finely chopped

1 Heat the oil in a small wok or a frying pan over medium heat. When the oil is lightly smoking but not too hot, gently add the garlic and stir now and then with a heatproof spatula. Try to spread out the garlic to ensure it cooks evenly. Once the garlic starts to turn a pale golden colour, remove the pan from the heat and continue stirring until the garlic is a light golden brown. Don't let it burn as this will make the garlic oil bitter.

2 Pour the garlic oil into a clean glass bottle or jar and store at room temperature for up to 2 weeks.

CILI JERUK

PICKLED GREEN CHILLI

This fresh pickled chilli is a versatile condiment that can be served with dishes, such as Wonton noodles, Mamak-style fried noodles or *Char kuey teow*, to name a few (see pages 72, 156 and 142). It's best made in advance to give the flavours time to develop, and can be stored in a clean jar in the fridge for up to a week.

MAKES ABOUT 300 G (10½ OZ)

160 ml (⅔ cup) white vinegar
½ teaspoon salt
2 tablespoons sugar
5–6 long green chillies, finely sliced

1 Combine the white vinegar, salt, sugar and 80 ml (⅓ cup) water in a small saucepan and bring to the boil over medium heat. Once the salt and sugar have dissolved, remove from the heat and set aside to cool completely.

2 Place the sliced chilli in a clean jar, then pour in the pickling liquid, making sure the chilli is completely covered. Leave it to cool slightly, then place in the fridge to chill for at least 2 hours before serving. The longer you leave it to pickle, the tastier it will be!

AIR ASAM

ASAM DIPPING SAUCE

With a nice balance of sweet, spicy and tangy flavours, this dipping sauce goes well with just about anything, especially Grilled fish (see page 149), seafood and meat.

MAKES ABOUT 600 ML (20½ FL OZ)

- 2.5 cm (1 in) piece toasted *belacan* (shrimp paste; see page 192)
- 375 ml (1½ cups) tamarind juice (see Note)
- 1 large red onion, finely diced
- 1 tomato, finely diced
- 1 teaspoon fish sauce
- 10 bird's eye chillies, finely sliced
- 1 tablespoon *kerisik* (toasted coconut paste)
- 2 tablespoons sugar, or to taste
- 1 teaspoon salt, or to taste

1 Stir the *belacan* into the tamarind juice until well combined.

2 Add the onion, tomato, fish sauce, chilli and *kerisik* and mix well. Season to taste with sugar and salt. Store in a glass jar or bottle in the fridge for up to a week.

Note

To make tamarind juice, add 2 tablespoons tamarind paste to 375 ml (1½ cups) water and mix until combined.

BOKWA SUI

PICKLED PAPAYA

The Nyonyas in Penang are partial to sour-tasting food, which is why tamarind and lime are often used in their cooking. However, the key to a good pickle is to have a good balance of flavours, namely sour, sweet, salty and spicy. This pickled papaya is enjoyed as a snack at any time of the day, in order to indulge their fondness for sour food outside of mealtimes.

SERVES 4

- 1.2 kg (2 lb 10 oz) unripe papaya (roughly 1 small papaya)
- 3 tablespoons salt
- 375 ml (1½ cups) white vinegar
- 220 g (1 cup) sugar

1 Peel the papaya and cut it into quarters, then cut into 1 cm (½ in) thick slices.

2 Place the papaya in a clean bowl, add the salt and and rub it in well. Set aside for 1 hour.

3 Meanwhile, combine the vinegar and sugar in a saucepan, bring to the boil and cook until the sugar has dissolved. Set aside to cool completely.

4 Rinse the salt off the papaya slices and drain in a colander, then pile into a clean glass jar. Fill the jar with the pickling liquid, making sure the papaya slices are completely covered. Close the lid and leave to pickle for at least 2 days before consuming. The pickled papaya keeps well at room temperature for a week. If stored in the fridge, it will last for up to one month.

SAMBAL HAE BEE

DRIED SHRIMP SAMBAL

Sambal hae bee (or *hae bee hiam* in Hokkien) is a really good accompaniment to many Nyonya dishes. This spicy and aromatic dried shrimp sambal is often eaten with Chilli flat noodles (see page 74), Chinese-style fried rice (see page 155), bread or used as a filling for savoury *pau* (steamed buns) and mini crispy spring rolls, a popular snack during Chinese New Year.

MAKES ABOUT 500 G (1 LB 2 OZ)

- 140 g (5 oz) dried shrimp, rinsed, soaked for 10 minutes, drained
- 3–4 red shallots, peeled
- 5 garlic cloves, peeled
- 20 g (¾ oz/about 30) dried chillies, seeded, rinsed, soaked in water for 15 minutes, drained
- 80 ml (⅓ cup) vegetable oil, plus extra if needed
- 2 teaspoons tamarind paste, or to taste
- 1 tablespoon sugar, or to taste

1 Process the softened dried shrimp and 2–3 tablespoons water in a blender or food processor to a coarse paste. Remove and set aside.

2 Add the shallot, garlic and dried chillies to the blender or processor and blitz to a coarse paste. Again, add 2–3 tablespoons water if needed to loosen the mixture.

3 Heat the oil in a wok or a frying pan over medium heat and stir-fry the chilli paste for about 10 minutes until fragrant and the oil has separated. Add the dried shrimp paste and stir-fry for another 5 minutes. Stir in the tamarind and sugar, then taste and adjust if necessary. The flavour should be a good balance of spicy, sweet, sour and salty.

4 Continue cooking the sambal for another 30 minutes, stirring constantly to make sure it doesn't stick to the wok or pan. Add a little more oil if the texture is too dry. Remove from the heat and let the sambal cool completely, then transfer to a clean airtight jar and store in the fridge for up to 2 weeks.

1kg Net
AYAM BRAND™
CLOUET
1892

SAMBAL KELAPA

COCONUT CHUTNEY

Sambal kelapa (or *thengal thuvayal* in Tamil) makes a wonderful accompaniment to Savoury Indian pancakes (see page 38) and Beef dal curry (see page 88). Some people also love to add coconut chutney to their Mamak-style mixed rice (see page 152) to give a little 'kick' to this local dish favoured by Penangites.

MAKES ABOUT 250 G (9 OZ)

2 teaspoons vegetable oil
1 teaspoon mustard seeds
1 teaspoon *urad dal* (black lentils)
1 curry leaf sprig, leaves picked
2 dried red chillies, sliced, seeded and soaked in water for 15 minutes, drained well

Coconut paste

150 g (5½ oz) freshly grated coconut
2 long green chillies, seeded and roughly chopped
1.5 cm (½ in) piece ginger
4 red shallots
2 garlic cloves
2 curry leaf sprigs, leaves stripped
1 teaspoon tamarind paste
1 teaspoon salt, or to taste

1 To make the coconut paste, place all the ingredients in a blender or food processor and blend to a smooth paste. Set aside.

2 Heat the oil in a frying pan over medium heat, add the mustard seeds and sauté for 30 seconds. Add the *urad dal* and curry leaves and cook for another minute until the *urad dal* turns golden brown. Add the dried chilli and cook for another 1–2 minutes until fragrant.

3 Add the coconut paste and cook, stirring, for another 5–7 minutes until the oil has separated and the chutney is thick and aromatic. Remove from the heat and allow the chutney to cool in the pan.

4 Transfer to an airtight container or a glass jar and store in the fridge for up to 2 weeks.

ACAR AWAK

NYONYA SPICY PICKLED VEGETABLES

Just like kimchi to Koreans and chutney to Indians, the people of Penang love to serve their rice dishes with *acar awak* or simply enjoy the pickled vegetables on their own. Packed with vibrant sweet, sour and spicy flavours, it just gets better and better with time.

MAKES ABOUT 2 KG (4 LB 6 OZ)

500 g (1 lb 2 oz) long cucumbers, halved lengthways, seeds removed, then cut into 4 cm (1½ in) long strips

1 large carrot, peeled and cut into 4 cm (1½ in) long strips

salt

450 ml (15 fl oz) white vinegar

200 g (7 oz) cabbage, roughly chopped

200 g (7 oz) snake (yard-long) beans, cut into 4 cm (1½ in) long lengths

120 ml (4 fl oz) vegetable oil

180 g (6½ oz) sugar

100 g (3½ oz) roasted peanuts, coarsely ground

200 g (7 oz) peeled pineapple, cut into small pieces

toasted white sesame seeds, to garnish

Spice paste

10 long red chillies, seeded and roughly chopped

5 dried chillies, soaked in water for 15 minutes, drained

10 red shallots, peeled and roughly chopped

5 garlic cloves, peeled

2 teaspoons ground turmeric

2 teaspoons ground galangal

3 roasted candlenuts (see page 192), coarsely pounded

3 tablespoons coriander seeds

20 g (¾ oz) toasted *belacan* (shrimp paste; see page 192)

1 Put the cucumber and carrot strips in a bowl, add 1 tablespoon salt and gently toss to combine. Leave for 30 minutes, then rinse the salt off the vegetable strips. Drain and squeeze out the excess water (this helps to retain crunchiness).

2 Bring a large saucepan of water to the boil and add 250 ml (1 cup) of the vinegar and a pinch of salt. Separately blanch the carrot, cabbage and beans for 2–3 minutes, then remove with a slotted spoon and refresh in a bowl of iced water. Drain well, then spread out the vegetables on a tray and leave to dry for 1 hour (another trick to retain crunchiness).

3 To make the spice paste, place all the ingredients in a blender or food processor and blitz to a smooth paste.

4 Heat the oil in a large wok over medium–low heat, add the spice paste and cook for 15 minutes or until fragrant and the oil has separated. Remove from the heat.

5 Stir in the sugar, 1 teaspoon salt and the remaining vinegar, then add the ground peanuts and mix well. Add the blanched vegetables, cucumber and pineapple and stir until combined.

6 *Acar awak* can be served straight away, but it's best to scoop it into an airtight container and leave overnight in the fridge to further develop the flavours. It will keep for up to 2 weeks. Serve garnished with toasted sesame seeds.

JELATAH

MALAY-STYLE VEGETABLE MEDLEY

Made with pineapple and cucumber, *jelatah* is a fresh vegetable medley full of sweet, sour and spicy flavours. Unlike conventional pickled vegetables, *jelatah* is best eaten fresh to maintain its crunchy texture. It goes beautifully with tomato rice (see page 95), Turmeric rice (see page 33) and many other dishes.

MAKES ABOUT 1.4 KG (3 LB 1 OZ)

- 1 long cucumber, peeled, halved and finely sliced
- 1 pineapple, skin removed, quartered and finely sliced
- 1 red onion, finely sliced
- 1 long red chilli, seeded and finely sliced
- 2 tablespoons sugar
- 1 teaspoon salt
- juice of 1 lime
- 1 tablespoon white vinegar

1 Place the cucumber, pineapple, onion and chilli in a large bowl and mix well. Add the sugar, salt, lime juice and vinegar and toss everything together.

2 Cover and store in the fridge until you are ready to serve. Store any left-over *jelatah* in an airtight container in the fridge for up to 2 days.

Note

For hassle-free preparation, tinned pineapple may be used instead of fresh, particularly if they are not at their seasonal best. The tin juices make a good substitute for the sugar too.

STOK AYAM

CHICKEN STOCK

This basic chicken stock is great in dishes like Tomato rice (see page 95) and as a broth for Chinese-style fondue (see page 150). By adding additional ingredients to the stock, you can use it as a base to make Penang white curry laksa (see page 64) or soup to accompany rice or noodle dishes like Chilli flat noodles (see page 74).

MAKES ABOUT 1 LITRE (4 CUPS)

- 1 kg (2 lb 3 oz) chicken bones or carcasses
- 2 garlic cloves, finely chopped
- 2 tablespoons grated ginger
- pinch of salt

1 Place the chicken bones, garlic, ginger, salt and 2 litres (8 cups) water in a large stockpot. Make sure the water completely covers the chicken.

2 Bring to the boil over high heat, then reduce the heat to low and simmer for 1 hour or until the stock has reduced and has a rich umami flavour. Strain through a fine-mesh sieve, discarding the solids, and transfer to an airtight container. The stock can be stored in the fridge for up to 3 days or in the freezer for up to 6 months.

Notes

You can replace the chicken bones with a whole chicken (about 1.2 kg/2 lb 10 oz) or chicken pieces (about 12 pieces) if you are planning to use the stock to make chicken rice (see page 62) or any other dish requiring chicken meat.

Because this stock freezes well, it's worth doubling or tripling the quantities and storing the excess in the freezer for a quick meal another time.

STOK UDANG

PRAWN STOCK

This is a good way to utilise every part of the prawn. Using the head and shells will give you a rich umami broth base to make just about any Malaysian dish you desire.

MAKES ABOUT 1 LITRE (4 CUPS)

- 1 tablespoon vegetable oil
- 3 garlic cloves, finely sliced
- 200 g (7 oz) prawn (shrimp) heads and shells

1 Heat the oil in a stockpot over medium-high heat, add the garlic and cook until lightly golden. Add the prawn heads and shells and stir until fragrant.

2 Pour in 2 litres (8 cups) water, bring to the boil and boil for 5 minutes. Reduce the heat to low and simmer gently for 1 hour or until the liquid has reduced by half. Remove from the heat. Strain through a fine-mesh sieve, discarding the solids, and transfer to an airtight container. The stock can be stored in the fridge for up to 3 days or in the freezer for up to 2 weeks.

HOMEMADE SOY MILK

Walk down any street or through any market in Penang and you will easily find hawkers selling soy milk and Soy milk pudding (see page 48), both made fresh daily. The great thing is, you have the option to buy it unsweetened or sweetened with palm or white sugar syrup. Here we show you how to make the unsweetened version.

MAKES 2 LITRES (8 CUPS)

185 g (1 cup) dried soybeans
2 pandan leaves, knotted and torn

1 Rinse the soybeans well, then place in a bowl with 500 ml (2 cups) water and soak at room temperature for at least 6 hours, or overnight if time permits. Drain.

2 Transfer half the soaked beans to a blender, add 750 ml (3 cups) water and blend until smooth. Pour the blended mixture into a bowl, then repeat this step with the remaining soybeans.

3 Line a saucepan with a single layer of muslin, then pour in the blended soybean mixture. Squeeze the liquid through the cloth into the pan, discarding the solids.

4 Add the pandan leaves to the soy milk and bring to the boil over medium heat. Once it comes to the boil, remove from the heat and let it cool completely. Discard the pandan leaves. Fresh soy milk will keep in the fridge for up to 5 days. To extend its longevity by another week or so, boil the milk again before storing it.

Note
Soy milk is sensitive to grease, which can make the milk spoil more quickly. Please ensure all the equipment is clean before making the milk.

KEDAI MOTOR KUAN YEE
ROCK OIL
Made In England Since 1928

alpro
FARMASI
ALPRO
大专药剂
KINI DI
LEBUH
CHULIA
(Berdekatan Balai Bomba)
013.362.3923
LEBUH CHULIA
Chulia St
10200 P.PINANG

KUAH KACANG

PEANUT SAUCE

This homemade peanut sauce has an amazing rich flavour and makes a particularly good dipping sauce for Chinese-style fondue (see page 150) or Prawn fritters (see page 100). Just like curry, this sauce tastes even better the next day.

MAKES ABOUT 500 ML (2 CUPS)

- 3 tablespoons vegetable oil
- 1 tablespoon Malaysian chilli paste (see page 170)
- 1 lemongrass stalk, white part only, bruised
- 1.5 cm (½ in) piece galangal, peeled (optional)
- 2½ tablespoons soft brown sugar
- 1 teaspoon ground coriander
- 140 g (1 cup) ground dry-roasted peanuts
- 1 tablespoon tamarind paste
- 1 tablespoon *kecap manis*
- ½ teaspoon salt, or to taste

1 Heat the oil in a medium saucepan over medium heat. Add the chilli paste and stir-fry for 1–2 minutes until aromatic. Add the lemongrass, galangal, brown sugar and coriander and stir-fry for another 30 seconds.

2 Stir in the ground peanuts, tamarind paste, *kecap manis* and up to 125 ml (½ cup) water. Season to taste with salt.

3 Reduce the heat to medium-low heat and cook, stirring constantly, for 5–10 minutes until the sauce has thickened to your desired consistency and the oil has separated. Remove from the heat and leave to cool at room temperature. Store in an airtight container in the fridge for up to 5 days or in the freezer for up to 3 months.

HAINANESE KAYA

CARAMEL COCONUT JAM

Most *kopitiams* (coffee shops) in Penang are owned by Hainanese people, which is why it's common to see Hainanese-style *kaya* toast (see page 18) on their menus. While the texture of the Hainanese *kaya* is a bit runnier than the regular *kaya*, it has a stronger coconut flavour and pairs beautifully with the fluffy charred Hainanese bread.

MAKES ABOUT 500 ML (2 CUPS)

3 eggs

200 g (7 oz) caster (superfine) sugar, plus 60 g (2 oz) extra

250 ml (1 cup) coconut milk

3 pandan leaves, knotted

1 Crack the eggs into a mixing bowl and whisk in the sugar until combined. Add the coconut milk and stir well, then strain the mixture through a fine-mesh sieve into a stainless steel bowl and add the pandan leaves.

2 Set the bowl over a saucepan of simmering water over medium heat for 7–10 minutes, stirring occasionally, until the mixture starts to warm and thicken.

3 Reduce the heat to the lowest setting and stir often to prevent any lumps forming. After about 10 minutes the jam should be thick enough to coat the back of a wooden spoon. Remove the bowl from the pan and stir constantly for another minute. Set aside.

4 Tip the extra sugar into a clean heavy-based saucepan over medium heat and add 1 teaspoon water. Without stirring, let the sugar dissolve and turn into an amber caramel, then quickly drizzle it into the jam mixture and mix well to combine.

5 Set aside to cool completely, then place the jam in an airtight jar. Store in the fridge for up to one month.

GLOSSARY

This is a list of commonly used and potentially hard-to-find ingredients outside of Malaysia. These ingredients can be sourced from Asian grocery stores specialising in Southeast Asian ingredients, at supermarkets or online.

Agar agar

A vegan substitute for gelatine, agar agar is made from red-purple marine algae. It is sold in powder, strand or flake form and is used to make jellies, puddings and custards.

Almond gum

An edible resin obtained from the sweet almond tree, almond gum is known to be a natural coolant for the body. It is widely used in drinks and Chinese traditional medicine.

Ang kwe flour

This mung bean flour is ground to a similar fineness as cornflour (cornstarch) and the two are often used interchangeably in cooking. *Ang kwe* flour is commonly used in Malaysian desserts, such as *cendol*, as the flour helps to yield a soft, stringy texture.

Banana leaves

Large green leaves cut from the banana tree. Banana leaves are waterproof and pliable, and versatile enough to be used for cooking, wrapping ingredients and serving food. They impart a subtle sweet aroma to a dish when steamed or grilled.

Basil seeds

In Malaysia, edible basil seeds are often used in drinks and desserts. These black and tear-shaped seeds are rich in protein as well as being a good source of fibre. Often, confused with chia seeds, you should also soak them first before consuming.

Belacan

This essential ingredient – also known as fermented shrimp paste – is a staple in Peranakan and Malay cuisine. *Belacan* is made from krill (tiny shrimp-like crustaceans) that have been salted, dried and fermented, which yield its deep salty-umami taste. Raw *belacan* should be toasted in a dry frying pan before using for best results.

Betel leaves

Aside from their culinary uses, these peppery leaves, with their distinct herby bitterness, are an integral part of Malaysian culture where they are used in prayer and wedding offerings, as well as being an antiseptic and stimulant. Betel leaves are rarely eaten alone, but they make an excellent addition to dishes, such as *nasi ulam* (herbed rice).

Butterfly pea flower

Also known as *bunga telang*, this flower is widely used in Peranakan cuisine as a natural blue food colouring for desserts and rice. These days, butterfly pea flowers usually come in dried or powdered form and can easily be sourced from Asian grocery stores.

Candlenuts

Large round nuts that closely resemble macadamias in appearance and texture, candlenuts are a key ingredient in Malaysian cooking, where they are regularly used as a thickener and a flavour and texture enhancer in sauce-based dishes like curry, *rendang* and sambal. Candlenuts should never be eaten raw as they are mildly toxic, so cook them for at least 15 minutes at 120°C (250°F) or above to help reduce their toxic effect and bitterness.

Chestnuts

An edible nut that comes from the same family as the beech tree. Bitter when raw, roasting chestnuts gives them a delicate and subtle sweet flavour.

Coconut milk and coconut cream

Coconut is an important ingredient in Malaysian cuisine, and one of its most important by-products is the opaque and milky-white liquid that is extracted from the grated pulp of matured coconuts. Coconut cream is much thicker and richer in consistency than coconut milk. Both come in liquid and dehydrated forms.

Dried anchovies

Known as *ikan bilis* in Malay, these tiny dried white anchovies are an essential ingredient in Malaysian cooking. They are normally added to stir-fries and sambals or eaten as a side dish as part of *nasi lemak*. These salty dried anchovies can be eaten raw, but are most delicious fried in oil until crisp.

Dried shrimp

With a unique umami taste, dried shrimp have been sundried until shrunk to thumbnail size. It is a regular ingredient in Malaysian dishes, such as *hae bee* sambal, and can be purchased from Asian grocery stores.

Dried sole fish

Also known as dried flounder, dried sole fish is used to enhance the umami taste in soups, broths and wonton fillings. It is normally sold in dried or powdered form and can be purchased from Asian grocery stores.

Duck eggs (salted)

Made by soaking duck eggs in brine, salted duck eggs are usually boiled or steamed before being peeled and eaten as a condiment to porridge or added to stir-fries. When boiled, the egg white has a sharp, salty taste; whereas the orange-red yolk is less salty, and rich and fatty in flavour.

Freshly grated coconut

Widely used in sweet and savoury dishes, freshly grated coconut is extracted from the coconut pulp using a special tool. Look for it in the frozen aisle at your local Asian grocery store.

Ghee

Widely used in Malay and Indian cooking, ghee is a clarified butter used to cook spice-based dishes or flavoured rice.

Ginkgo nuts

The mildly sweet kernel from the fruit of the ginkgo tree, ginkgo nuts are widely used in Chinese cooking to make soup or *tong sui*. Although highly nutritious, they are slightly toxic and, therefore, should be eaten in moderation.

Hae kor

Also known as *petis udang* in Malay or simply shrimp paste, *hae kor* is a salty-sweet and fragrant condiment frequently added to fruit and vegetable salads or used as a topping on *asam laksa*. The perfect accompaniment to sweet and savoury dishes, *hae kor* can be also combined with other ingredients to make an umami-rich sauce.

Jicama

Sometimes referred to as yam bean or *sengkuang* in Malay, the jicama is a globe-shaped root vegetable with a golden brown skin and a starchy white interior. Crunchy and sweet, jicamas are commonly eaten raw and are often added to fruit and vegetable salads, such as *pasembur*.

Kerisik

This important ingredient is widely used in Southeast Asian cooking to achieve the signature nutty, caramelised flavour in dishes, such as *kerabu* (Asian salad) and *rendang*. Known as 'coconut butter', *kerisik* is made from grated coconut pulp, which is then toasted and ground into a paste.

Laksa noodles

Thick rice noodles with a springy and chewy texture, laksa noodles are usually sold fresh or dried. Look for them in the refrigerated section or noodle aisle of your local Asian grocery store.

Limestone water

This natural mineral water is made using pink limestone. In Malaysian cooking, it is added to batters to make crispy fried foods and pastries. Limestone water is available at Asian grocery stores in liquid or paste form.

Malaysian curry powder

The ratio of spices used to make Malaysian curry powder – cinnamon, star anise, cardamom, cloves – will differ depending on the protein (seafood, meat or chicken) you are adding to curries, soups or sauces.

Malva nuts

Native to Southeast Asia, malva nuts are commonly used in traditional medicine to cool the body, treat sore throat infections and relieve coughs. They are tasteless, apart from a hint of sweetness, and are usually mixed with red dates, licorice and chrysanthemum flower to make sweet soups such as the Chinese *tong sui*.

Osmanthus

Also known as sweet osmanthus, the flowers of this evergreen shrub have a slight apricot flavour. Osmanthus is commonly used to flavour teas and desserts.

Pandan leaves

Known as the 'Asian vanilla' (some say the leaves have a sweet vanilla smell, while others claim they can taste nutty almond notes), pandan leaves are widely used to add flavour and colour to sweet and savoury Malaysian dishes. They are sold at Asian grocery stores where they can be purchased fresh, frozen or dried.

Petai

Also known as 'stink beans', *petai* are flat, edible beans that grow in clusters, hanging from the branches of the *Parkia speciosa* tree. The beans are wrapped in a tough outer skin of twisted pods that need to be peeled before cooking. *Petai* are usually eaten raw with sambal or added to savoury dishes. Although the beans have a pungent smell, they are packed with a nutty flavour and are a local favourite among Malaysians.

Sago

An edible starch extracted from the spongy centre of tropical palm stems, sago look like small, white, opaque pearls. In Malaysian cooking, it is normally cooked in water or coconut milk and is widely used in sweet and savoury dishes.

Snow fungus

A white and almost translucent fungus, snow fungus has little taste. When rehydrated and cooked it has a crunchy and gelatinous texture which absorbs flavour.

Tamarind

The fruit pod of the tamarind tree, the flavour of tamarind ranges from sour and sweet to tangy and tart. Tamarind is sold as a pulp or a paste or in dried slices.

Torch ginger flower

Also known as *bunga kantan*, torch ginger flower is an indispensable ingredient in Malay and Peranakan cuisines. The large pinkish buds are commonly used to zest up curries and stews, but they can also be eaten raw as part of an aromatic garnish for salads, rice and soups.

Turmeric leaves

These small to medium oblong leaves are used extensively as an aromatic herb in Malaysian cooking. They have a neutral aroma in fresh form, but once cut and pounded, they release a distinctive tart flavour with notes of grass and mint. Turmeric leaves can also be used to impart floral, pungent and gingery flavours, with slightly bitter undertones, to dishes.

RM8-00
100 Gms
RM 8.00
100 Gms

ABOUT THE AUTHORS

Aim and Ahmad are a Melbourne-based duo who grew up in Malaysia. Throughout their childhood, they often travelled to Penang to visit friends and family, and, of course, to savour the island's humble yet incredible food scene. Even now as adults, they find themselves returning regularly. For them, Penang will always feel like home.

Aim is a postgraduate researcher at RMIT University, specialising in mechanical engineering and renewable energy. She's also a freelance travel and food photographer, working with a broad range of clients. Her lifelong love of Southeast Asian cooking – especially the flavours of her homeland – has been a constant since childhood.

Ahmad is a Malaysian-born chef with a passion for good food, thoughtful flavours and genuine hospitality. He began his culinary journey in Melbourne in 2012, building a strong foundation in modern Australian cuisine while staying rooted in his cultural heritage.

Together, Aim and Ahmad founded Eat Scintilla, a creative platform blending modern Australian cooking techniques with the bold, vibrant flavours of Southeast Asia.

After nearly a decade in Melbourne, they've taken the leap and are now on a roving culinary adventure, hosting pop-ups and collaborations across Indonesia, Japan, Thailand, Malaysia and beyond. Along the way, they've been reconnecting with chefs, creatives and kindred spirits in the hospitality scene, all while sharing an ever evolving take on the food they love.

ACKNOWLEDGEMENTS

Writing a cookbook that explores the Penang food scene, along with its rich history, has been a wonderful journey for us, and we are so grateful to have met so many great and amazing people in this special part of Malaysia.

To our Smith Street Books' family, thank you so much for trusting us and giving us this golden opportunity to write this cookbook. To Paul McNally and Hannah Koelmeyer, thank you for making our dream come true. Until today, we still cannot believe how lucky we are to have come across both of you. To Lucy Heaver, thank you so much for being so patient with us and guiding us all the way to the finish line. Thank you as well to Megan Cuthbert and Ana Jacobsen.

To Rachel Carter, our editor, thank you so much for giving the right 'voice' to our words and for being awesome at what you do. We really appreciate it! A very big thank you to graphic designer Murray Batten, photographer Georgia Gold, and food stylist Deb Kaloper, for helping us make the cookbook of our dreams.

To our amazing Melbourne family, you know who you are. Thank you so much for always supporting us and being excited at our endeavours.

To Milly, we love you always and forever.

Finally, to our lovely family, a heartfelt thank you for always supporting us.

SYARIKAT
BOON WAH
文華綢莊
BOON WAH
BOON WAH

INDEX

D

M

N

O

P

R

S

Published in 2026 by Smith Street Books
Naarm | Melbourne | Australia
smithstreetbooks.com

Distributed outside of ANZ, North & Latin America by
Thames & Hudson Ltd., 6-24 Britannia Street, London, WC1X 9JD
thamesandhudson.com

EU Authorised Representative: Interart S.A.R.L.
19 rue Charles Auray, 93500 Pantin, Paris, France
productsafety@thameshudson.co.uk; www.interart.fr

ISBN: 978-1-9232-3975-3

Smith Street Books respectfully acknowledges the Wurundjeri People of the Kulin Nation, who are the Traditional Owners of the land on which we work, and we pay our respects to their Elders past and present.

Publisher: Hannah Koelmeyer and Megan Cuthbert
Design: Murray Batten
Typesetter: Megan Ellis
Food photographer: Georgia Gold
Food stylist: Deborah Kaloper
Proofreader: Ana Jacobsen
Production manager: Aisling Coughlan

Printed & bound in China by C&C Offset Printing Co., Ltd.

Book 433
10 9 8 7 6 5 4 3 2 1

Recipes in this book have previously appeared in *Penang Local*, published by Smith Street Books in 2021.